McGRAW-HILL INSURANCE SERIES
RALPH H. BLANCHARD, *Editor*

LLOYD'S

McGRAW-HILL INSURANCE SERIES

Ralph H. Blanchard, *Editor*

LLOYD'S

C. E. GOLDING, LL.D., F.C.I.I.
and
D. KING-PAGE

FIRST EDITION

McGRAW-HILL BOOK COMPANY, Inc.

NEW YORK   TORONTO   LONDON

1952

LLOYD'S

Library of Congress Catalog Card Number: 51-12565

PREFACE

Much has been written about the great institution known as
Lloyd's, but the greater part of this is concerned with the
historical aspect of the subject. The purpose of this book is
to set out in detail the way in which business is transacted
at Lloyd's, including sufficient history to make an intelligi-
ble story, but otherwise concentrating on showing the practical working of its affairs at the present time.

It is strange that while "Lloyd's" is a household word all
over the world, comparatively few people, even in the
United Kingdom, have any idea of how business is carried
on there; how the Corporation is organized; or how it serves
the shipping and other major industries not only of the
United Kingdom but the world at large.

It is the endeavour of the writers of this book to place on
record not only some account of how business is carried on
at Lloyd's but also of the services which this corporation
renders not only to those who do business there but to shipping and commerce in general and even to the private individual. Fundamentally Lloyd's never changes. On broad lines
business is carried on at Lloyd's today very much as it was
in Edward Lloyd's Coffee House in Great Tower Street in
the 1680's, but in detail Lloyd's is ever changing. Many still
alive have seen the development of Lloyd's from a market
almost solely concerned in marine insurance into one where

practically every form of insurance is carried on and, indeed, where many of the modern types of non-marine business originated.

It may be that even while this book is in publication some new development will take place in the detail of business transacted at Lloyd's. More than one has taken place since it was commenced. Nevertheless, every care has been taken to make this book an accurate record of the practical side of Lloyd's, and the authors acknowledge fully the help they have received in this respect from the Committee of Lloyd's and the staff of the corporation. It is emphasized, however, that this work is the sole responsibility of its authors, and no official authority whatever is claimed for it. It is hoped, however, that it will fill a useful place in the literature on Lloyd's.

C. E. GOLDING
D. KING-PAGE

LONDON, ENGLAND
December, 1951

CONTENTS

Chapter 1. THE ORIGIN OF LLOYD'S

The purpose of this book is to set out in a comprehensive manner the nature of that great insurance institution in London known as Lloyd's, to show how it came into being, to explain how it operates, and to make plain how its work is carried on.

This chapter will be devoted to the early history of Lloyd's, with a description of how it gradually developed from its first beginnings to the finished product of the present time. Lloyd's did not come into existence as the result of any deliberate act. At no time did any body of businessmen come together and say, "Let us form an insurance association with such and such powers and with a membership according to a predetermined plan." No such definite decision was ever taken, for Lloyd's grew up gradually and by a natural process of evolution. Those who began it probably had no idea where it was to lead and they certainly could not have foreseen to what it was destined to grow.

Marine Insurance

To understand the way in which Lloyd's came into existence, it is necessary to go back to the conditions of business life which were in vogue in London in the sixteenth and seventeenth centuries, and to examine the origins of the insurance business. The records of insurance in its earliest development are unfortunately not complete or very reliable, but it seems reasonably clear that marine insurance was es-

1

tablished in a form comparable with modern patterns at a stage earlier than any other form of insurance. No records of fire insurance, for example, appear earlier than the great fire of London in 1666. Life assurance on a scientific basis came nearly a century after that when the Equitable Life Assurance Society was formed in 1746, while accident insurance was unknown in England before 1840, and does not appear to have been practised in any other country prior to that year. But marine insurance was certainly practised long before any of the dates referred to, not of course with the pitch of perfection which it has attained today, but at least on lines which are recognisable as the direct forerunner of modern methods.

There are records to show that marine-insurance policies were issued as far back as the fourteenth century. There was a chamber of insurance in Bruges in 1310 through which merchants could insure their goods whilst at sea. In 1347 a policy was issued to insure a cargo on board the ship *Santa Clara* while on a voyage from Genoa to Majorca. This old policy was described by William D. Winter in a pamphlet published by the Insurance Society of New York, and it is probable that this is the earliest record extant of a marine-insurance transaction. In the Bodleian Library at the University of Oxford there is a copy of a marine policy dated 15th February 1613 on the ship *Tiger*. It seems to be established that during the sixteenth and seventeenth centuries policies were issued from time to time covering marine risks, because the few which remain on record today must be representative of a great many others which have been lost.

But none of these policies was issued by an insurance company, for no marine companies were in business before the year 1720. The insurance granted under all the policies which have been traced was made by one or more individuals, and it may be taken as demonstrated that all such insurances issued before 1700 were of that nature. The business appears to have been undertaken by merchants as a kind of side line, though it was not restricted to merchants, for the famous diarist Samuel Pepys appears, from entries in his diary in 1666, to have had an interest in a marine-insurance venture. It was this early system of insurance which gave rise to the term "underwriter," a word which was used to show that a man had *written* his name *under* the statement of the subject matter and terms of the insurance, that is to say, at the foot of the policy. The original and only meaning of the term underwriter was thus the person who made himself liable for the insurance. It may be well to remember this in view of the extension of meaning which has been attached to the word in modern usage. Nowadays the term "underwriter" has come to mean the official of the insurance company or other institution who considers the risks offered for insurance, weighs up their merits, decides as to their acceptability, and fixes the rate of premium appropriate to the risk. This particular aspect of insurance is called the practice of underwriting and is no longer associated with the liability assumed by the insurers except in an indirect way. In reference to Lloyd's underwriters, the term is used even more loosely; its exact meaning in that connection will be explained in a later chapter.

The Coffee Houses

At the time referred to, London was already an old and populous city, with a well-established business community.

The merchants and other businessmen who were willing to add to their income by underwriting marine risks had become numerous and had their offices or other places of business in the city. But then, as now, men did not spend all their day in their offices and they formed the habit of congregating for social intercourse and refreshment in taverns and coffee houses. Inns and taverns had been established in great numbers in the city of London from time immemorial, but the first coffee house appears to have been opened by one Pasqua Rosee in 1652 in St. Michael's Alley, Cornhill. The coffee houses offered certain advantages, chiefly the fact that they were quieter, more orderly, more suitable for conversation among sober, respectable businessmen. In any event they quickly multiplied and became an accepted part of the business life of London, being situated in the courts and alleys round about the Royal Exchange.[1] The merchants practising marine insurance were amongst those who frequented these coffee houses, and without any particular intention, they tended to gravitate towards one or two special coffee houses. This was because men with the same interests naturally come together, but no doubt men followed an established usage, so that their friends might know where to find them. The Royal Exchange, which stood at the time on a site very near that occupied by the present building, was largely used for the business of underwriting, and resort to the coffee houses was made particularly for the purpose of obtaining news—news of

[1] The Royal Exchange is a building in the City of London first erected in the reign of Queen Elizabeth for the use of merchants and others having business in the City. The Royal Exchange Assurance Corporation takes its name from the fact that its offices were and still are situated in that building.

the events of the day, or of the political developments of the moment, news of the movements of shipping and of other matters in which the merchants were interested.

Lloyd's Coffee House. Amongst the coffee houses in existence at that time was one kept by Edward Lloyd, which appears to have been set up in Tower Street, London, about the year 1688 and to have been moved to new premises at 16, Lombard Street in 1691. From that comparatively obscure London citizen has been derived the name of Lloyd's, which is known and respected all over the world. Edward Lloyd himself could not possibly have guessed at the lustre which was to be attached to his name, for he laid none of the actual foundations upon which the modern Lloyd's has been reared. Edward Lloyd opened a coffee house pure and simple with no thought of catering particularly to merchants engaged in insurance. His purpose was to supply coffee to all who cared to ask for it, and in this respect his resembled many other coffee houses, of greater reputation at that time, whose names by the accident of fortune have long since passed from memory. It is true that Edward Lloyd appears always to have been interested in shipping. For some time he issued a news sheet giving the movements of shipping, while other news of general interest was disseminated from his house as from many others. His house was also frequently used for the public auction of ships.

For these reasons it was natural that those who were interested in marine-insurance matters frequently resorted to Edward Lloyd's coffee house, where they were likely to hear news of importance to them. But Lloyd had no kind of monopoly of their attendance, and they were to be found also in many other places. It is certain that up to the time of the formation of the two chartered marine companies in 1720, the Royal Exchange Assurance and the London Assurance, the business of marine insurance had never been associated with Lloyd's coffee house more than with any other. That association came about by accident rather than by design; by one of those strange chances of fashion which cannot be foreseen or explained. Certainly up to 1720 the marine underwriters had either to be sought at the Royal Exchange, or in their offices, or in any one of the coffee houses or other places of refreshment where they might be found.

It should be emphasised that the early underwriters were not engaged solely in insurance, but merely carried it on as a side line to their ordinary business as merchants or shipowners or as the case might be. An interesting example of what was done in those days is furnished by the story of John Walter, the founder of *The Times* newspaper. He was originally a coal merchant, who as a side line underwrote marine insurance on coal shipments. This business prospered, and in course of time he came to Lloyd's, though subsequently his business failed. He then began business as a printer, which led him in due course to found *The Times*.

In an indirect way the monopoly granted to the two chartered companies in 1720 seems to have led to the formation of the early nucleus of Lloyd's. The charters granted to the two corporations gave them an absolute monopoly, so as to prohibit any other corporations, societies, or partnerships from engaging in the business of marine insurance. But a special proviso was inserted saving the rights of "private or particular persons," which meant that private underwriters could continue to carry on the business which had been developing during the previous century. In this saving clause, and indeed in all the protracted negotiations leading up to the granting of the two Royal Charters, there is no mention of Lloyd's Coffee House. This fact furnishes a further proof that it had attained no particular significance in the transaction of marine insurance at that time.

But as soon as the private underwriters came into competition with the chartered companies, the inconvenience of their being scattered about the City became apparent. The two companies could always be found in their offices, and it became imperative that some common meeting place should be available in which the private underwriters could be found with reasonable certainty. As has been explained, Lloyd's Coffee House had by this time acquired an extensive shipping and mercantile connection; it had been frequented by many underwriters for many years past, and as the need for a closer association arose, Lloyd's seems to have been more and more used for that purpose, not all at once or even exclusively, but with a steady persistence which finally led to the complete concentration of the business. This does not mean that any official association existed between Lloyd's and the underwriters who met there. Edward Lloyd himself had died in 1713, but the Coffee House was continued in his name and was used by the underwriters as a meeting place, and so far as they were concerned, nothing more. Nevertheless the use of Lloyd's Coffee House as a place for underwriters continued in increasing measure during the first half of the eighteenth century, and it is easy to understand how the longer it went on the more firmly the custom became established. In the first place all those connected with marine insurance, whether as underwriters, or as merchants and brokers with ships to insure, would get to know that Lloyd's was the place to go to, to get the business done. Secondly those who were successively masters of the Coffee House— Edward Lloyd himself, then William Newton, his son-in-law, followed in turn by Samuel Shepherd, Thomas Jemson, Richard Baker, and Samuel Saunders—were quick to appreciate the character of the business which was growing up around them, and to make what provisions they could to advance its interests. The establishment itself was of the highest class; it had become a recognised auction mart for ships and prize cargoes; in 1734 *Lloyd's List* was first published, and in 1760 the Register Book Society was established. These developments created the right atmosphere in which marine insurance could flourish, and it may be supposed that the underwriters readily recognised that fact. They would feel at home in such surroundings, and their habit of congregating there would become more and more firmly fixed.

New Lloyd's Coffee House. This state of affairs went on till the year 1769, when there came a change sufficiently significant to be marked as a milestone in the evolution of Lloyd's, the split among the customers of the Coffee House in Lombard Street which led to the setting up of a rival concern under the name of New Lloyd's Coffee House.

It seems probable that this came about through some deterioration in the management of the original Lloyd's. On the death of Samuel Saunders in 1763, the Coffee House passed to his brother-in-law Thomas Lawrence, who did not attend to the business himself, but put in as manager one Charles Waller who had previously been head waiter. The reason for the break which followed in 1769 is not altogether clear, though it appears that at about that time an undesirable speculative and gambling element had penetrated

into the business, which gave strong offence to the more
reputable members of the insurance fraternity and was posi-
tively injurious to their business. For this reason they determined to break away from this unpleasant association and
set up a new coffee house in which they could pursue their
business on more statisfactory lines. For this purpose they
did not approach the proprietors of the original Coffee House
but selected one of the waiters, by name Thomas Fielding,
and arranged with him to open a new coffee house in Pope's
Head Alley. On Monday, March 20th, 1769, the following
notice appeared in the *Public Advertiser:*

> To the Merchants in general, Owners and Freighters of
> Ships, Insurance Brokers etc. etc. Thomas Fielding, Waiter
> from Lloyd's Coffee House begs leave to acquaint them that
> his House in Pope's Head Alley Lombard Street, is now
> genteely fitted up and will be opened for the reception of
> Gentlemen, Merchants etc. Tomorrow the 21st instant by the
> name of New Lloyd's Coffee House, where he hopes to re-
> ceive their favours which shall be gratefully acknowledged
> by
>
> Their most obliged humble servant
Tho. Fielding

Whether or not those merchants who had supported Fielding gave him any financial assistance is not clear, though he
must have been assured of the patronage of a substantial
number of them. In any event the new venture proved to
be a success and was able to obtain from the Post Office
the grant of the right to issue *Lloyd's List.* Yet the older
concern did not go down without a struggle, and for some
years there were two coffee houses and two *Lloyd's Lists,*
with a fierce rivalry between them. But the newer concern

contained the best and most stable elements in the insurance organisation, and the power and influence of the older concern, so far as concerned the business of marine insurance, steadily and inevitably declined, whilst the influence of the New Lloyd's Coffee House in Pope's Head Alley as steadily advanced. It was from this new coffee house that the coming together of individuals for the purpose of marine underwriting developed into the organised society which resulted in the Lloyd's of the present day.

Lloyd's Founded

The first step in that direction was taken in 1771, only 2 years after Thomas Fielding had set up his new coffee house, for on the 13th December in that year, 79 merchants, underwriters, and brokers signed an agreement as follows:

> We the underwriters do agree to pay our several subscriptions into the Bank of England in the names of a Committee to be chosen by ballot for the building a New Lloyd's Coffee House.

Each subscriber made himself responsible for £100, and this agreement marked a definite stage in the growth of Lloyd's. It meant the first formal association between the underwriters; they put their own money into the concern; they were no longer merely individual men resorting to someone else's place of business; they meant to have a place of their own, even though the coffee-house character of the premises was to be retained. For these reasons the year 1771 is to be regarded as the date of the foundation of Lloyd's because it was in that year that its members first bound themselves together by agreement and the first common action was taken between them. In 1772 the Committee of Lloyd's was first set up to manage its affairs. At first these subscribers were not all underwriters, though all had a common interest in marine insurance. The present position as between underwriters and brokers at Lloyd's did not become settled until much later, about the middle of the nineteenth century.

The Royal Exchange

Some time elapsed before the Committee was able to secure the new premises which they desired, for it was not until March, 1774, that they obtained suitable premises in the Royal Exchange, where they were destined to remain until their removal to the present new building in Leadenhall Street in 1928. The premises in the Royal Exchange were fitted out as a coffee house, but at the expense of the subscribers. Thomas Fielding was installed as Master and was to be entitled to make what profit he could out of the services rendered to the subscribers, but subject to their general control. In effect Fielding and his assistants became the servants of the subscribers, and attended to all their wants. The attendants at Lloyd's are to this day known as "waiters," a term which has come down unaltered from the days when the business was conducted in the Coffee House.

By the time the move to the Royal Exchange was made the work had increased greatly. The original 79 subscribers had increased to 179 by April, 1774, and many additions were made every year. A subscribers' room had been set up apart from the public coffee room, and it soon became necessary to reserve this room for the subscribers' sole use, as otherwise it became so congested that business was almost impossible. Subscriptions in those days were made by lump sums,

£20 per head being paid by the original subscribers, which was afterwards reduced by £5 to £15 each. This subscription gave a life membership of Lloyd's, admission to the subscribers' room, and a right to vote at the general meetings. This arrangement compares very favourably with the practice of the present day.[1] It was at this time that the first daily record of ships lost and ships safely arrived began to be kept. A book bound in green vellum was instituted for this purpose and was known familiarly as "The Book." This was of the greatest assistance to the subscribers and gave them a considerable advantage over those underwriters who, not being subscribers to the new Lloyd's, still carried on their business in the public room of Lloyd's itself or in the other coffee houses about the city. It is easy to see how the superior organisation of the new Lloyd's, with its more reliable and up-to-date information, must have gradually ousted from the business those who stood apart from it. This would come, not from any desire on the part of the promoters of Lloyd's to establish a monopoly, but because it was clearly through such an organisation as theirs that the business could best be transacted. This organisation had progressed to such an extent that as early as 1779 the subscribers to Lloyd's were able to draw up a printed form of policy which was accepted as the standard form and which differs in only a few particulars from that in use at the present day.

The older coffee house founded by Edward Lloyd in Lombard Street appears to have continued in business until 1785 or thereabouts, in which year the premises were described in the rate book as empty. The institution at the

[1] See Chap. 2.

Royal Exchange was still called "New Lloyd's" until about 1794, and the daily list was *New Lloyd's List* until 1789. From those dates, however, the word "new" was dropped, and at some stage the words "coffee house" also disappeared. Thus was created and set in motion the institution which we know today under the single word "Lloyd's."

Early Development

It must be emphasised, however, that the development of Lloyd's as an entity was slow and proceeded only by gradual stages. It is clear that the pioneers were in no hurry; they did not set out to fashion any kind of corporate undertaking, with a set of rules and regulations to govern their procedure. They were content to work for the moment to settle only such matters as were immediately pressing, and they took no particular thought for the future. Indeed at the time of the movement to the Royal Exchange in 1774 only one rule was made which affected the possibility of future developments. This was to the effect that any 12 subscribers should have the power to call a general meeting of the subscribers for the purpose of making any new regulations or alterations, giving 7 days' notice to the Committee. Though it does not appear that this rule was invoked very often in the years immediately following, it provided the machinery for development and fulfilled that purpose in due course. From 1774 down to the commencement of the war with France in 1793, the development of Lloyd's was devoted only to an increase in the number of its subscribers and was not concerned with any growth in its organisation or with any expansion of its corporate functions. There was at that time no

control exercised by the Committee either over the subscribers themselves or over the conditions upon which they
carried on their business.

The effect of the French wars was to throw a very heavy
liability onto the underwriters and involve them in serious
losses arising out of war conditions. At the same time there
came a great influx of business, and in spite of various crises
which were bound to occur in such circumstances, by the
time the war was over, which so far as the seas were concerned may be taken as about 1810, there was no doubt that
the leading underwriters came out with their credit completely unshaken. Lloyd's as a whole had grown, in consequence, both in size and in financial strength and influence.
Moreover, the strenuous time through which they had passed
went a long way to draw the underwriters together and to
establish the atmosphere calculated to further the conversion
of a large number of individual underwriters into one co-
herent body of men, with common interests and engaged
in a common business.

One effect of this was to give a predominant position to
marine insurance in the business done at Lloyd's. At first
the subscribers had a number of different interests, of which
marine underwriting was only one, but gradually the leaders amongst the subscribers came to regard marine insurance
as their first concern until in time this became the only business carried on. In the development of Lloyd's at that time
two men exerted an outstanding influence. These were John
Julius Angerstein and Brook Watson. Angerstein—who is
sometimes called the Father of Lloyd's—lived from 1735 to
1823. He was a man of great charm and force of character,
a great patron of the arts, and a friend of the leaders in

political and social circles. He was both broker and underwriter and conducted his business on lines which commanded
the respect and admiration of all with whom he came in contact. Whether he was ever actually Chairman of Lloyd's
does not appear to be known, but he took an active part in
many of its important developments. He was mainly instrumental in arranging the removal to the Royal Exchange in
1774 and by his enterprise and integrity as an underwriter
and broker did much to raise the prestige of Lloyd's and to
enhance its authority.

Brook Watson, born in the same year as Angerstein, had
a more varied career. In his time he served a military career,
became a merchant in the city, was a director of the Bank of
England, a member of Parliament, and Lord Mayor of London. He was a member of the original Committee of Lloyd's
set up in 1772 and so remained till his death in 1807. He was
undoubtedly Chairman of the Committee from 1797 to 1806,
and a great proportion of the credit for the development of
Lloyd's as an institution, which took place during that particular period, is due to him. It must be remembered that
those were war years, and during that time Lloyd's was in
close and continuous correspondence with the Admiralty
on matters affecting their common interests. In many cases
also direct contact was established between Lloyd's and the
masters of ships, in a way which seems a little strange to
modern ideas. It illustrates the growing importance of Lloyd's
that a great Government department such as the Admiralty
should condescend to establish contacts of this nature.

All such correspondence was originally passed through
the Masters, *i.e.*, the proprietors, of the Coffee House who
were charged with duties of this nature; but this proved un-

satisfactory in course of time, and eventually a Secretary to the Committee was appointed. This did not come however until 1804 when John Bennett, Jr., was appointed to that post. The corporate spirit had been growing before that and was considerably promoted by the leading part played by the underwriters in organising public subscriptions in aid of the dependants of seamen killed in the war. The administration of these funds brought the Committee of Lloyd's into contact with the Admiralty and ship's officers and men and brought a letter of appreciation from Lord Nelson himself. In connection with these matters the Committee had to meet much more frequently than had formerly been necessary. The importance of these activities lies in their effect on the minds of the subscribers, who began to regard themselves more and more as members of one institution and not so much as isolated individual units. The most important of these charitable activities on the part of the subscribers was probably the Patriotic Fund, established in 1803, which had as its object "the encouragement and relief of those who may be engaged in the defence of the country and who may suffer in the common cause." This fund was started by Lloyd's with a transfer of £20,000 from their corporate funds. The fact that they could do this bears testimony to the progress which had by that time been made in the establishment of the corporate spirit. The Patriotic Fund developed to such an extent that it soon became a national affair and passed out of the control of Lloyd's as such, though many of the leading underwriters were on the management committee.

The increase in the activities of the Committee of Lloyd's was shown by the fact that from 1780 to 1793 only 18 meetings were recorded, but in 1795 there were 15, and from

1800 onwards the average rose to between 12 and 20 each year. In 1796 the subscribers passed a resolution that two ordinary general meetings should be held in each year, at midsummer and Christmas. At one of these general meetings, presumably that held at Christmas, the Committee were required to present an annual report and statement of accounts. It is surprising that this had not been done before, but it is obviously an important landmark in the development of Lloyd's as a corporate body, not only as showing that the members had begun to realise their common interests, but also because those interests had become of sufficient magnitude to warrant an annual report.

Membership Qualifications

Having reached this stage it occasions no surprise that in 1800 there was instituted for the first time a qualification test to be imposed on those applying for membership, a very necessary step if the character of the developing institution was to be preserved. Previously anybody could be admitted as a subscriber, if he desired to underwrite a little marine insurance or to have access to the confidential information supplied. It did not matter what other activities he might have, nor how subordinate to his main business his marine underwriting might be. If he was prepared to pay the subscription of £15 the Masters were bound to admit him. This is understandable when it is remembered that Lloyd's grew out of the Coffee House. It would not have been possible for the Master of the Coffee House to exclude any particular patron merely on the ground that he was or was not engaged in this or that class of business. The fact that the early subscribers to Lloyd's were admitted by the

Masters shows how this original idea had been carried on. Now, however, the Committee decided to alter this, and at a general meeting held on the 2nd April, 1800, at which Brook Watson presided, a resolution was passed providing that ". . . only merchants, bankers, underwriters and insurance brokers should in future be admitted as subscribers." The classes of businessmen mentioned in this resolution show a particular feature which has always been characteristic of Lloyd's, that some of the subscribers, *i.e.*, bankers and merchants, employ others to write on their behalf, while others, *i.e.*, the underwriters, write on their own account or as agents for others, but so that the underwriting is their sole business. This aspect of the constitution of Lloyd's is fundamental and is more fully dealt with in a later chapter.

A further provision made at the same time was that every candidate for election must be recommended in writing by at least six subscribers, and in practice every election was therefore made formally by the Committee. The election was a personal one and no longer applied to all the partners in a firm, unless each was elected separately in his own name. Ivory tickets bearing the names of subscribers or their permitted substitutes were issued to be shown at the doors of the subscribing rooms. These simple regulations had a great effect for they enabled the existing members through their Committee to control the growth of their own organisation, and it became possible to carry out effectively what had always been the intention, to permit the use of the subscribers' rooms to subscribers and no one else. Where a thing grows by such slow and imperceptible stages as the corporate entity of Lloyd's, it is not easy to say which particular fact exercised the most influence, but the resolutions of 1800 undoubtedly were of the highest practical importance. The result of all these matters was to bring into being an institution very different from that which was set up when Lloyd's New Coffee House was established in 1774. In the short space of 30 years Lloyd's had become a great public institution whose interests were consulted, whose assistance was sought, and whose advice was sometimes taken by the government.

Crisis of 1810–1811

Progress such as this was bound to breed envy, and Lloyd's was not without its enemies, who would have welcomed an opportunity to curtail its growing influence. These got their chance, in an indirect way in 1810 and 1811, though the attack was made as an offshoot of something different. In those years bills were promoted in Parliament to break the monopoly in marine-insurance companies which had been held since 1720 by the Royal Exchange Assurance and the London Assurance. A certain number of London merchants put forward an idea for the flotation of a big new company with a nominal capital of £5,000,000 to carry on marine insurance, and this of course could not be done without repeal of the monopoly. This was made the opportunity for a concerted attack on Lloyd's and on its methods, which led to something of a crisis in its affairs. A Select Committee was appointed by Parliament to consider the matter, and it is to be feared that the report of that Committee was not characterized by that impartiality which the importance of the subject demanded, for much of the evidence in Lloyd's favour appears to have been ignored or glossed over. However, the first bill introduced in 1810 was dropped by its promoters, and a second bill brought in in 1811 was defeated by one vote. The situation was thus saved for the time being, and since there can be no doubt that the real purpose of the promoters of these bills was to destroy Lloyd's, the outcome must be regarded as entirely satisfactory.

Reorganisation

Following this shock and perhaps because of it, a more far-reaching reorganisation of Lloyd's was soon put in hand, the urge for which came from the members themselves. The issue which led to this was a small one in itself and arose from dissatisfaction with the way in which certain intelligence communicated by or on behalf of the Admiralty had been prepared for publication to the subscribers by the Secretary. Various committees were set up to consider what regulations should be laid down for the management of the House in the future. At a general meeting on the 23rd May, 1811, 42 subscribers were nominated from whom a committee of 21 were elected by ballot. Since in effect the proceedings amounted to a vote of censure on the old House Committee, its members refused to serve on the new Committee, but the new Committee entered on the task they had set themselves with considerable energy and after due inquiry made a draft of a set of rules and regulations. The most important of these new regulations provided for the following:

Subscribers. The qualifications for new subscribers were reaffirmed on the lines laid down in 1800, so as to restrict these to merchants, bankers, traders, underwriters, or insurance brokers. The method of election was prescribed, and the subscription was increased to

£25 on election and an annual subscription of 4 guineas.

Committee. The Committee should consist of 12 members, three of whom were to retire by rotation each year and to be eligible for re-election a year later. The Committee was to elect a Chairman and three other members as a Treasury Committee to be trustees of the funds.

Secretary. John Bennett, Jr., was confirmed in his appointment as Secretary and was granted a salary of £200 a year.

General Meetings. Any resolution to alter the rules and regulations was to be confirmed at a subsequent general meeting before it could be acted upon.

Appointment of Agents. The Committee was empowered to appoint agents in any port to act on behalf of the general body of subscribers. This was an innovation of great importance for it represented the beginning of the vast network of Lloyd's agencies which has played so vital a part in the development of its activities.[1]

The new rules and regulations were rounded off and consolidated by a Trust Deed drawn up in August, 1811, and signed by all the subscribers, which formally vested in the Treasury Committee the corporate funds of the subscribers and bound the subscribers individually to observe all the rules and regulations then made or thereafter to be made. This deed gave legal effect to the By-laws and became the formal instrument uniting the subscribers into one business association.

One of the principal figures behind this new development

[1] The growth and work of Lloyd's agents are dealt with in detail in Chap. 6.

was Joseph Marryat, M.P., who had taken a prominent part in the struggle of 1810, and who was now appointed Chairman, a position which he occupied till his death in 1824. The mark left by Marryat on the growth of Lloyd's was almost as great as those of his distinguished predecessors. Lloyd's had now acquired a constitution, with a code of By-laws and a regular routine for carrying out its corporate affairs. The period from 1811 to 1823 was one of steady consolidation, and the procedure became regularised by force of repetition so as to combine in one society what had hitherto been only an assembly of individual underwriters.[1] This led in course of time to an alteration in the system by which the Masters of the Coffee House had exercised a great deal of control. They had received not only all the revenues of the Coffee House, but also the annual subscriptions of the members. Their accounts as between the Coffee House and the subscribers were inextricably mixed, a system which could not continue indefinitely. An alteration was made in 1823, when the Committee took into its own hands the financial arrangements relating to the affairs of the subscribers, increased the powers of the Secretary, and put the Masters under his control. From that time the Masters were concerned only with the Coffee House, which still remained, and their authority was greatly reduced in consequence,

---

[1] From this time and perhaps even earlier, it became the custom to refer to the "Society of Lloyd's," though there was nothing formal about it. In the Trust Deed of 1811 it is referred to as the "Establishment or Society held at Lloyd's," while in Lloyd's Act 1871 the word Society is officially used. As the Society was incorporated under this Act, it has since then been commonly referred to as the Corporation of Lloyd's.

though the position of Master was not actually abolished until 1837. Thereafter the Coffee House was controlled by a head waiter who was a servant of the Society and responsible to the Committee. For many years previously the Coffee House, though open to the public, had been frequented mainly by ship masters or others interested in shipping and had begun to be called the Captains' Room as far back as 1812. After the abolition of the post of Master, the Coffee House as such disappeared, and the room remained for the use of members and their friends, as the Captains' Room so well known to modern frequenters of Lloyd's.

Repeal of the Monopoly

The attempt made in 1810 and 1811 to break the marine-insurance-company monopoly was renewed in 1824 and this time successfully. In that year an Act was passed through Parliament, by which the monopoly held since 1720 by the Royal Exchange Assurance and London Assurance was repealed. It must be understood that this was not a private Act aimed specifically at those two corporations, but a public Act making it lawful for insurance companies to engage in marine insurance. The immediate result was the formation in 1824 of two new marine companies, the Alliance Marine and the Indemnity. This Act was as strenuously opposed by Lloyd's as had been the abortive attempts of 1810 and 1811, and many were the direful effects which it was prophesied would result to the underwriters by the passing of the Act. None of these gloomy forebodings was in fact realised, and it was soon clear that the placing of marine insurance on a free-for-all footing only went to strengthen Lloyd's and to make that institution more nearly permanent

and complete. Looking back on the matter from today, it is
difficult to imagine how it could ever have been thought
otherwise. However, the position was not accepted by Lloyd's
at once, and there was at first no friendly co-operation with
the new marine companies on the same lines as that which
had existed for more than a century between Lloyd's and
the two old marine corporations. The new companies were
not supplied with Lloyd's shipping intelligence or given the
full benefits of Lloyd's agency system. The co-operation between Lloyd's and the marine-insurance-company market
which exists today did not come into full force until 1840,
when the information at Lloyd's disposal was first supplied
to companies outside the two corporations.

Depression and Prosperity

The period of ten years or so following 1824 was a time of
depression and gloom in the development of Lloyd's. For
various reasons, one of which was the end of the Napoleonic
war period, there was a serious diminution in the volume
of insurance offered. Joseph Marryat died in 1824, and his
loss was severely felt. Dissension arose between the Committee and the members, which was overcome only with
considerable difficulty. To cap all, in 1834 John Bennett, who
for 30 years had controlled the affairs of Lloyd's as Secretary,
died at the comparatively early age of 56, leaving behind
him a gap which it was extremely difficult to fill. However,
these were but growing pains in the development of the institution, and the period of depression was successfully sur-
mounted. Under the chairmanship of G. R. Robinson, which
began in January, 1834, an era of revival set in. Confidence
was restored, business improved, the dissensions between

the Committee and the members died down, and renewed progress was made.

A setback was experienced in 1838 when the Royal Exchange was completely destroyed by fire, including all the office accommodation then occupied by Lloyd's. Fortunately a great many of the records were preserved, but a heavy loss was incurred in the destruction of the file of *Lloyd's List* and the original Trust Deed of 1811. As this document was the foundation upon which association between the members legally rested, it was necessary to replace it immediately. This was done by drawing up a new Trust Deed, in brief terms with a copy of the old deed annexed, which was signed by the subscribers. New quarters were found in South Sea House, at the corner of Threadneedle Street and Bishopsgate, and the temporary interruption of the smooth working of the business was overcome. Lloyd's remained at that address until the new Royal Exchange was built. This is the building which now stands in the City of London, and it was formally opened by Queen Victoria on the 28th October, 1844. The new offices leased to Lloyd's were much superior to the old in spaciousness and construction. They extended over 11,000 square feet compared with 7,500 square feet in the old building, but in fact the seating accommodation was reduced, there being room for only 258 underwriters, against 320 before.

On the return to the Royal Exchange in 1844 the opportunity was taken to make a further revision in the By-laws, a matter which had been under the consideration of a special committee set up for that purpose in 1838. The principal effect of the new By-laws was to divide the establishment into two classes, members and annual subscribers; this was the first time this distinction appeared. Both classes paid an annual subscription of £4.4.–, but only members were required to pay the entrance fee of £25. Only members could sit on the Committee or vote at general meetings. Every underwriter in the room was required to become a member, whether he underwrote in his own name or employed someone else to do it for him. The effect of this change was to confirm the control of Lloyd's more effectively in the hands of the underwriters.

From this time onwards the business transacted at Lloyd's began steadily to expand, not because of the adventitious aid of any period of warfare but on account of the great development of trade and commerce which took place during the middle years of the nineteenth century. This was the time of the introduction of steam and the invention of mechanical means of carrying out manufacturing processes. The great improvement in the telegraph as a method of rapid communication had brought a great advantage to the business of Lloyd's. The membership of Lloyd's grew accordingly and had increased from 945 subscribers in 1843 to over 1,250 members and annual subscribers by December, 1846. Nevertheless, owing to heavy expenses, the finances of the Society had got into a bad way and something had to be done to increase the revenue. Also, the seating accommodation had become totally inadequate. The latter point was met eventually by a rearrangement of the rooms and by taking in other offices adjacent in the building. Various attempts were made to improve the revenue, and this was finally done on a permanent basis in 1859. In that year by a resolution in general meeting the institution was divided into three categories, viz., underwriting members, non-underwriting members, and annual subscribers. Underwriting members were required to pay £50 entrance fee, 12 guineas annual subscription, and 5 guineas for each substitute's ticket. Substitutes were authorised representatives of the underwriters, admitted to Lloyd's by the authority of the Committee to act there on behalf of their principals. Non-underwriting members paid £25 entrance fee and 4 guineas annual subscription, while annual subscribers paid 5 guineas a year. These changes had the effect of still further consolidating the predominance of the underwriting interests and played a part in restricting the activities of Lloyd's to marine-insurance business, though they were subsequently extended to non-marine. The number of non-underwriting members steadily fell away, while the number of underwriting members increased. The annual subscribers were mainly brokers, who now play an important part in the working of Lloyd's.[1]

It was about this time that the system of giving security by the members of Lloyd's to the Committee began to develop. This point of practice in the development of the business is more fully dealt with in Chapter 2. Its historical interest lies in the fact that it shows how the idea of corporate responsibility was growing.

Incorporation

Up to this time Lloyd's had been a purely private association, governed in certain of its aspects by a committee, but possessing no constitution with the force of law behind it or giving it legal power to act in a corporate capacity. It became obvious in course of time that this position was not entirely satisfactory, and a remedy was sought. In 1871 Parliament

[1] See Chap. 3.

passed Lloyd's Act by which the members were incorporated
into one body, with perpetual succession and a corporate
seal. The objects of the Society were set out in the Act as follows:

1. To carry on the business of marine insurance by members of the Society.
2. The protection of the interests of members of the Society in respect of shipping and cargoes and freight.
3. The collection publication and diffusion of intelligence
and information with respect to shipping.

The Act provided for the formation of the Committee of
Lloyd's and the manner in which it was to be elected. The
voting powers of the members were determined, and a set
of rules was promulgated for the governance of the members in their relations with the corporate body set up by
the Act. The Corporation was given powers to deal with its
corporate funds, to purchase real or personal property, and
generally to exercise the powers vested in a body incorporated under an Act of Parliament.

No great radical change was made in the methods by
which the Society of Lloyd's was administered. In fact
special care was taken to see that the old Trust Deed and
By-laws were adhered to as closely as possible and that the
freedom of members in the conduct of their business was
preserved. The effect of the Act was to grant to the Society
the recognition of the legislature, to make it an incorporated
body with all the statutory powers as defined in its Act.
Whereas before the Society had consisted of a number of
individuals who came together for a common purpose and
who submitted to rules and regulations by common consent,

it now became a corporate entity with rules possessing the
force of law and with a government on a recognised legal
footing. It may usefully be emphasised that this had no effect on the discretion of the underwriting members as to
how they should conduct their business, this being entirely
their private affair. The Corporation of Lloyd's set up by
the Act controlled that part of the affairs which was common
to all and which required control and regulation for the
common good. This dual aspect of Lloyd's under which the
Corporation controls the corporate affairs and the members
pursue their private business affairs, each apart and distinct
from the other, is a fundamental characteristic of the Society,
which must be grasped before the nature of the institution
can be properly understood.

Further Acts of Parliament have since been passed where
experience showed that extended powers were necessary. By
Lloyd's Act 1888 its powers were enlarged to include the collection, publication, and diffusion of intelligence and information generally, without the qualifying words "with respect to shipping."

By Lloyd's Act 1911 an important extension was made
to the objects of the Society, removing the restriction to marine insurance contained in the Act of 1871. The objects
of the Society were set out afresh in the Act of 1911 as follows:

1. The carrying on by members of the Society of the business of insurance of every description including guarantee
business.

2. The advancement and protection of the interests of
members of the Society in connection with the business carried on by them as members of the Society and in respect of

shipping and cargoes and freight and other insurable property or insurance interests or otherwise.

3. The collection publication and diffusion of intelligence
and information.

4. The doing of all things incidental or conducive to the
fulfilment of the objects of the Society.

Finally Lloyd's Act 1925 conferred additional powers of
making By-laws and amended the Act of 1871 in certain particulars relating to the election of the Committee.

Some doubt has arisen in lay minds as to the proper way
of writing the name of Lloyd's, whether with or without the
apostrophe. To resolve this doubt it may here be stated that
the apostrophe is always required. The name is derived from
Edward Lloyd's Coffee House. His name was Lloyd, and the
possessive case was required to denote that it was his coffee
house. When in process of time, the reference to the Coffee
House was discontinued, the form Lloyd's still remained, and
this expression has now received legislative sanction, since it
is so set out in the relevant statutes.

Chapter 2. THE UNDERWRITERS

The business carried on at Lloyd's is the acceptance of insurance, and this is done by the *underwriters*. Some description of the underwriters and the manner in which they function is necessary for a proper understanding of the purpose of Lloyd's. It is well again to emphasise the distinction which exists between the Society of Lloyd's as it is officially called, although this term is not often used, or the Corporation of Lloyd's, *i.e.*, the corporate body which controls its common affairs, and the individual underwriters, who make up the principal part of the membership. The members belong to the Corporation and submit to its control in so far as that control may properly be exercised, but they pursue their business activities entirely on their own account. The underwriters are the direct descendants of those early city men who came together in Edward Lloyd's Coffee House to transact marine insurance, and they have retained the independent position in their business activities which belonged to them from the beginning.

The underwriters are the men who actually make themselves responsible for the risks which are insured at Lloyd's. The expression "at Lloyd's" may be noted. We do not say "insured with Lloyd's" for that might imply that the risk was accepted by the Corporation of Lloyd's. This is not so. The risks are insured with the underwriters, who are to be found at Lloyd's, and so are said to be insured at Lloyd's. In theory

31

it would be possible for every underwriting member of Lloyd's to attend each day for the purpose of accepting insurances, but in practice this is not done. For one thing *The Room* is not large enough to accommodate all the underwriting members. The Room is the name given to the large business hall which occupies the ground floor of Lloyd's building in Leadenhall Street, a term which has been hallowed by long years of usage. For another thing, not every underwriter possesses the specialised knowledge of insurance which would be required to enable him to accept risks on his own behalf on a safe and businesslike basis.

The Syndicates

Altogether there are about 2,700 underwriting members of Lloyd's, who have joined together into a smaller number of *Syndicates*. These Syndicates are not all of the same size. The members of a Syndicate are called "Names," possibly because theirs are the names which appear on the policy. They are all underwriting members, even if they do not actually underwrite. They are personally responsible for the insurances accepted and are parties to the contract of insurance between themselves and their insured. Every such Syndicate is represented by one man who has a seat in The Room and is called the underwriting agent. He is the man with insurance knowledge, with the ability to weigh up the risks offered to him and to quote a proper rate therefor. He is a man of considerable experience, as indeed he must be, for the financial welfare of the members of the Syndicate, which he represents, depends solely upon the skill with which he underwrites the business offered to him. He may be himself an underwriting member of Lloyd's and may be included as one of the Names in his Syndicate, or he may be merely an agent for his Syndicate, without any direct responsibility for a share of the business he accepts. For convenience it is usual to speak of the underwriting members composing the Syndicate as "Names," and of the underwriting agent as "the underwriter," and this nomenclature is hereafter adopted in this book.

Each Syndicate divides its total responsibility between its members in certain prearranged shares. These shares are usually in fractions, which must of course total up to a complete unit. When the underwriter accepts a risk he accepts it for his whole Syndicate, so that every member receives his allotted share. This is a fundamental feature of the business operations of Lloyd's. The underwriter cannot interest some of his Names on a risk and leave others off. Each is entitled to his due share of every risk written. To take a simple example, a Syndicate may consist of five Names, each having a one-fifth share. If the underwriter accepts £1,000 on a risk, each name will be responsible for £200. In fact Syndicates constructed in this simple way are not very common. Before a man can be elected as an underwriting member, or Name, various formalities in regard to deposits and guarantees have to be complied with, and the burden of these very properly varies with the proportion of the risk which the Name is to assume. In most Syndicates there are predominant partners with a substantial share of the business—men of wealth and position well able to take a large share of the risks—while other members may have much smaller shares according to their means and position in life. The fractions of the whole Syndicate set against the name of each member will accordingly vary greatly and may sometimes be subdivided into quite small proportions, subject always to the invariable proviso that the total must add up to one complete whole.

Several Liability

A very important feature of this division of risks amongst the members of a Syndicate is that their liability is not joint but several. This means that each is liable for his own share but is not liable for the share of any of the other members of his Syndicate. On the policy this is given effect by the words, "each for himself and not one for another." The rule as to several liability has been a fundamental feature of the business done at Lloyd's from the very beginning of that institution. It came into being through men coming together in one place for their own convenience, but not at all for the purpose of joining their separate business activities into one common venture. The formation of underwriters into Syndicates in no way affected this principle, which has always been most jealously guarded. For the same reason there has always been a firm rule against partnerships amongst underwriters. This rule had in fact been enforced on Lloyd's by the Act of 1720 which granted a monopoly in marine insurance to the Royal Exchange Assurance and The London Assurance and prohibited such insurance not only by any other corporation, but also by any partnership firm. Only "private and particular persons" were exempt from this prohibition, and only in that way could Lloyd's conduct marine insurance. The By-law passed on the 11th August, 1824, after the breakdown in that year of the old marine-insurance monopoly, affirmed this principle in the following terms:

No subscriber shall underwrite policies of insurance within the Rooms of this House in partnership forms, or otherwise than in his own name, or in that of one individual for each respective sum subscribed.

This rule was expressed in legal form in Lloyd's Act 1871, and its continuity is thus assured. It maintains the personal aspect of the business of Lloyd's by means of which insurances are placed with individuals. This is the main distinction between insurance at Lloyd's and insurances placed with an insurance company.

Although it has been explained that, when an underwriter accepts a risk, he must accept it on behalf of his whole Syndicate, each member to receive his proper share, yet there is nothing to prevent the same underwriter from accepting business on behalf of more than one Syndicate, and in practice that is often done. In that case he is free to accept risks for either one Syndicate or more than one, as he pleases. He may accept the whole risk for one Syndicate, or divide it among his different Syndicates in any proportion he thinks proper. It is only when he has determined the amount to be given to each Syndicate that the rule applies by which every member of the Syndicate must have his proper share. This freedom to interest one Syndicate and not another in any given risk is necessary to carry out the methods of business as done at Lloyd's; for, as will be seen in a later chapter, the business has developed in such a way as to create specialised markets, so that certain classes of risk are placed mainly with Syndicates which specialise in those classes.

The Underwriter

Although the Names have to carry the risks accepted on

their behalf, a very great responsibility rests on the underwriter, for on his skill and ability depends the success of the venture which he undertakes on behalf of his Syndicate. The Names themselves are therefore dependent upon the soundness of their selection when they appoint their underwriting agent, for if they act unwisely in this matter, they may find themselves involved in heavy losses, the responsibility for which they cannot escape. Conversely, a wise appointment may bring them much prosperity and profit from their venture. So important an appointment must be well remunerated. The method of remuneration is of course a private matter between the Names and their agent, but usually the underwriter receives a fixed fee payable by each Name, which is quite independent of the results achieved on the business. This fee is generally quite modest, say £200 per annum for each Name, but for the major part of his remuneration the underwriter looks to his commission on the profits which he is able to earn, which is fixed at a percentage of the trading profits credited to the Syndicate. The system of remuneration by profit commission is well adapted to a business undertaking of this kind, for it fulfils the double purpose of giving the underwriter a share in a profit which owes its existence to his skill, and of promoting the underwriting of risks on a sound and cautious footing so as to ensure as far as possible that a profit will result.

Security

It remains now to be considered what is the nature of the security which stands behind an insurance effected with underwriters at Lloyd's and upon which the due performance of the obligations thereby undertaken depends. As soon as a risk has been accepted on behalf of a Name, that underwriting member becomes liable in respect thereof, and the liability runs not only against himself but also against his estate in the event of his death. This means that there is no limited liability at Lloyd's in the sense that the liability of the shareholders of a limited company is limited. Each Name at Lloyd's is liable for his obligations up to the full amount of his resources, whether being used in the business or being his own private means. This is of course the essence of private trading as distinguished from trading in the corporate capacity of a limited company and is one of the main distinctions between Lloyd's and the insurance companies. From this it follows that, if the funds of an underwriting member accumulated in the course of his trading proved insufficient to meet his liabilities, he would be liable to contribute his private funds to the extent required to make good any deficiency.

For these reasons, the election of any person as an underwriting member of Lloyd's is not a thing to be done lightly, for the good name and reputation of Lloyd's as a corporate entity must depend very largely on the manner in which the individual Names are able to meet their obligations. This fact has been clearly realised and is reflected in the various steps taken to see that only proper persons are elected as underwriting members and to ensure that due safeguards are provided for the carrying out of their obligations. Since this is a matter of primary importance in the affairs of Lloyd's, it may be well to set out the exact details of the financial security provided.

Whenever any person makes application for election as an underwriting member of Lloyd's he must obtain six existing members of Lloyd's to sign his application form and is required to fill in a statement giving full details in regard to any other business carried on by him and of his means, the amount of which must be certified by his bankers or accountants. It should be understood that many underwriting members of Lloyd's are engaged in other business activities, the nature of which must be disclosed.

In addition to giving these particulars the applicant must answer any inquiries which may be put to him by the Committee. The object of these inquiries is to satisfy the Committee that the applicant is a fit and proper person to be elected and is likely to be able to fulfil all the obligations he will incur. This is, however, only a preliminary proceeding, and by itself it would not be sufficient, for a man's financial position may change and what was satisfactory at the time of application might subsequently cease to be so. This was recognised many years ago, and the point was met by requiring the applicant to make a substantial deposit, to be held by the Committee on trust as security for his underwriting liabilities. This deposit must be made in the form of cash, or gilt-edged securities, so as to be readily negotiable if required. These securities are transferred into the name of the Committee of Lloyd's but the dividends thereon are paid to the underwriting member, always provided that he is not behind in meeting his liabilities.

This deposit was first made compulsory in 1870 when a rule was adopted under which all new members were required to make a deposit of £1,000 as a condition of election. The figure, though perhaps reasonable at the time, would not be adequate for the scale upon which most underwriting members conduct their business today, and the amount of deposit now required, while varying according to the character and volume of the business it is proposed to transact, will be regulated by the Committee and will usually be more substantial, the minimum being £5,000. In fixing the amount of deposit required, the Committee will take account of the applicant's private resources. It is not possible to lay down any definite rule on the point but a new member would not be likely to gain admittance unless he could show that he was possessed of free assets of at least £25,000 and that he was not engaged in any other business of a type likely to jeopardise those assets.

Before an applicant can be admitted to membership he will be required to submit himself to a personal interview with the Committee, with whom the decision rests. If the Committee approves his application he will be required to give an undertaking that his annual premium income shall not exceed a certain amount, for it is on that amount that the total security to be deposited by the applicant will be fixed by the Committee. The final stage in the election to membership is the payment by the applicant of an entrance fee, which goes to the Corporation of Lloyd's. The entrance fee was fixed at the time of the incorporation of Lloyd's in 1871 at £50 but this figure has since been increased by successive stages, until it now stands at not less than £500, except that in special cases it may be reduced to £250.

After the applicant has been elected as a member, it will be necessary for him to secure an underwriting agent to enable him to commence business, unless he decides to underwrite on his own behalf. In modern practice no underwriting member would commence to do business in his own name only, and it is not often that a new Syndicate is formed composed of a group of new members. Most of the new members elected nowadays join an existing Syndicate, either as an additional Name or to replace a Name who has either died or retired from business. In that case they will of course find their agents already appointed, and their participation in the business may begin from some convenient date to be arranged. It should be noted that the death of an underwriter brings his interest in his Syndicate to an immediate end. It is also open to an underwriter to retire from a Syndicate in accordance with the terms as to notice and the like contained in his agreement with his underwriting agent. In the event of a Name going out of a Syndicate by either death or retirement, an account would have to be struck of all business accepted up to the material date, for the deceased Name's estate or a retired Name himself remains liable for all such risks and is entitled to any profits which may eventually result therefrom.

Trust Funds. The security provided by a Name for the due performance of his obligations does not stop at the making of a deposit as above mentioned but is supplemented by the creation of a trust fund into which premiums are paid. In theory, as the Name accepts the responsibility for all insurances underwritten and the underwriter is merely an agent, it would be possible for the underwriter to pay over to his Name all premiums as he received them, and to call upon his Name for the payment of claims as they arose. In practice it is not done in that way, and it has long been compulsory on every underwriting member to pay all his premiums into a trust fund, set up under a trust deed, which provides that those premiums shall be used only for the payment of his underwriting liabilities. Only when the claims have been disposed of is the balance put at the disposition of the Name; all premiums must be fully earned, all claims paid or properly reserved for according to the system adopted at Lloyd's; and in effect the Name receives in cash only the earned profit.

There is a point of much advantage in the trust-fund system, for it prevents the premiums from becoming liable for the private debts of the Name. As the business of a Name is purely a private matter with no resemblance to a limited-liability company, the responsibility of the Name is unlimited up to the extent of his resources. This applies with equal force to any other business activity in which he may engage. In the absence of a trust fund, therefore, his assets no matter whence derived would be liable as a whole for any failure to meet his obligations and there would be no special protection open to those who had paid premiums for insurance. All creditors would have equal rights, so that unfortunate trading in other directions might result in the policyholders' being deprived of their security. The trust fund prevents this by giving the policyholders preferential rights under the trust deed while not taking away their rights against any other assets of the Name to make good any deficiency in the trust fund. It thus constitutes a valuable additional security. It makes the insurance side of the Name's affairs into a self-contained business not liable to be affected by any outside causes. The trust fund of each Name is administered by trustees and varies in amount according to the volume of business transacted by the Name, thereby in a practical way balancing assets against liabilities.

Audits. Before leaving the subject of the nature of the security offered by the Names for the due performance of the obligations which they assume, reference may be made

to the system of audit of underwriting accounts in vogue at
Lloyd's, for this has an important bearing on the soundness
of the business methods employed. It must be explained that
a Lloyd's Syndicate is in the nature of a private association
for a specific purpose. It is not a partnership because there
is no joint responsibility. It is not a public company and does
not fall within the provisions of any Act of Parliament
dealing with the business of a limited company. There is
therefore no obligation imposed on a Syndicate to prepare
its annual accounts in any particular manner or to deposit
them with any public authority for scrutiny. Of course no
business could be carried on without annual accounts, and
every underwriter must prepare a statement every year, if
only for the reason that he must show how the Syndicate's
affairs are progressing and what balances are available for
distribution. These figures used to be prepared by the underwriter, who accepted responsibility for their accuracy, and
they were not subject to audit by any independent firm of
chartered accountants. For many years the system was
worked in this way, and from the point of view of mere accuracy in the presentation of the figures, it worked well. But
the preparation of insurance accounts requires much more
than accuracy in putting forward the figures year by year.
It involves also the ability to estimate the amounts required
to provide for outstanding liabilities—liabilities for risks still
unexpired and for claims not yet settled—and it was to make
sure of the adequacy of the methods employed in this matter that *The Audit* was introduced in 1908. It is called The
Audit but in fact it is much more than an audit as applied,
for example, to the accounts of a public company. An audit,
as usually understood, means the checking by an independ-

ent firm of accountants of the figures submitted in the accounts as taken from the books of the company and as amplified by any explanations which may be called for. The Audit put into force at Lloyd's is more comprehensive than this and includes not merely the verification of the figures, but also a system of investigation into and control over the accounts and the invested funds of each Syndicate. For this reason the expression "The Audit" does not entirely convey what is meant, but it is always used and is well understood by all who practise business at Lloyd's. The methods by which the audit is conducted may be set out briefly as follows:

The underwriting accounts of each Syndicate as prepared by the underwriter are investigated each year by a certified accountant drawn from a panel set up by the Committee of Lloyd's and composed of accountancy firms of good standing and with the special experience necessary to deal with underwriting accounts.

The investigation includes not only the checking of the figures, but also an examination of the business of the Syndicate in accordance with rules laid down by the Committee of Lloyd's. These rules are designed to show whether the business is being carried on along sound lines, and whether the amounts carried to reserve are sufficient for their purpose. Thus if the trust fund falls below a certain ratio of the premium income the Names in the Syndicate must either provide out of their private resources a sum sufficient to make the trust fund up to the required ratio, or they must stop underwriting. The ratio is fixed at a figure high enough to give some margin of safety over what should normally be necessary to run off the liabilities. Where the Syndicate

carries on more than one class of business a different ratio
may be fixed for each separate class, since some may require more than others. For example, it will usually require
a larger percentage of the premiums to run off a third-party
business than it would for a fire business, for in third-party
business the claims come more slowly to settlement, and
accurate estimates are more difficult to fix in advance.

As a result of his investigation the accountant furnishes a
certificate to the Committee of Lloyd's that the Syndicate's
premiums are duly held in the trust fund and that the fund
is sufficient to meet the underwriting liabilities, apart from
any other assets which the Names possess. If the audit dis-
closes that an excessive part of the business has been reinsured, the Committee may inquire as to the soundness of
the reinsurers. This is a wise precaution, for the Syndicate
remains liable to its insured for the full amount of its indemnity and would have to meet its claims in full, even though
some of its reinsurers might fail to meet their obligations.

Governmental Regulation. An explanation of the methods
of keeping accounts used at Lloyd's is given in Chapter 4.
The certificate of the auditors, besides providing evidence
of the soundness or otherwise of the business carried on,
also enables the members of Lloyd's to comply with the requirements of the Assurance Companies Act 1909 as amended
by the Assurance Companies Act 1946.

The group of statutes cited as the Assurance Companies
Acts 1909 to 1946 regulate the carrying on of insurance business in Great Britain. Although the 1909 Act still remains in
force as the principal Act, it has been amended in certain
important ways by the 1946 Act. The principal Act applied
only to fire, life, personal-accident, workmen's-compensation,

and bond-investment business. Motor-insurance business was added to its scope by the Road Traffic Act 1930, and now by the 1946 Act marine, aviation, and transit insurances are also included, thus bringing within the regulations all the principal classes of insurance.

Originally much of the business transacted at Lloyd's fell outside the scope of the Act of 1909, and that Act did not apply in its entirety to the members. Although under the current group of Acts practically all the business done at Lloyd's is included, the members are still exempt from certain provisions of the Act in the same way as before, provided, however, that they comply with certain requirements particularly adapted to meet the conditions under which Lloyd's carries on business.

These requirements originally set forth in the eighth schedule to the principal Act have now been revised and are set out in Part II of the second schedule to the Act of 1946. The relevant extracts from the statute are as follows:

2. The Committee of Lloyd's and the managing body of an approved association, shall deposit every year with the Board of Trade a statement in such form as may be prescribed by regulations made by the Board summarising the extent and character of the assurance business done by its members in the twelve months to which the statement relates; and the said regulations may require the statement to deal separately with such classes or descriptions of business as may be specified in the regulations.

3. (1) As from such day as the Board of Trade [1] may by

---

[1] The Board of Trade is a department of the British Government which deals with trade, commerce, and industry in so far as these are controlled by statutory or Government regulations.

order appoint, there shall be substituted for the said Eighth
Schedule to the Principal Act the following Schedule:

EIGHTH SCHEDULE,

REQUIREMENTS TO BE COMPLIED WITH BY UNDERWRITERS
BEING MEMBERS OF LLOYD'S OR ANY OTHER ASSOCIATION
OF UNDERWRITERS APPROVED BY THE BOARD OF TRADE

1. (1) Every underwriter shall, in accordance with the
provisions of a trust deed approved by the Board of Trade,
carry to a trust fund all premiums received by him or on his
behalf in respect of any assurance business.

(2) Premiums received in respect of long term business
shall in no case be carried to the same trust fund under this
paragraph as premiums received in respect of general business, but the trust deed may provide for carrying the premiums received in respect of all or any classes of long term
business and all or any classes of general business either to
a common fund or to any number of separate funds.

2. (1) The accounts of every underwriter shall be audited
annually by an accountant approved by the Committee of
Lloyd's or the managing body of the association, as the case
may be, and the auditor shall furnish a certificate to the Committee or managing body and to the Board of Trade in such
form as the Board may by regulations prescribe.

(2) The said certificate shall in particular state whether in
the opinion of the auditor the value of the assets available to
meet the underwriter's liabilities in respect of assurance business is correctly shown in the accounts, and whether or not
that value is sufficient to meet the liabilities calculated—

(a) in the case of liabilities in respect of long term business, by an actuary; and

(b) in the case of other liabilities, by the auditor on a basis
approved by the Board of Trade.

(3) Where any liabilities of an underwriter are calculated

by an actuary under the last foregoing sub-paragraph, he shall furnish a certificate of the amount thereof to the Committee of Lloyd's or the managing body of the Association, as the case may be, and to the Board of Trade, and shall state in his certificate on what basis the calculation is made; and a copy of his certificate shall be annexed to the auditor's certificate.

3. (1) The underwriter shall, when required by the Committee of Lloyd's, or the managing body of the association, as the case may be, furnish to them such information as they may require for the purpose of preparing the statement as to the business done by its members which is to be deposited by them with the Board of Trade.

(2) The Board of Trade may make regulations providing for the manner in which deposits made, and premiums placed in a trust fund, under the provisions for which the Schedule set out in the foregoing sub-paragraph is to be substituted are to be dealt with on the said substitution taking effect, and for any other matters which appear to them to be incidental to or consequential on the said substitution; and the said regulations shall have the effect notwithstanding anything in any trust deed made for the purposes of those provisions.

The general effect of these regulations is to require the Committee of Lloyd's to make annually a summarised return of the amount of business done at Lloyd's and to require individual members to set up trust funds and to submit audited accounts. The Committee's return was a new feature provided by the 1946 Act, but the trust fund and audit of members had previously been required under the 1909 Act and had been done voluntarily for some years before that Act was passed. The intention of these provisions seems to be to give stability to the business and to ensure as far as possible correctness in carrying it out. In those respects this is only to give legal force to what had always been the guiding principle upon which business at Lloyd's is conducted.

Additional security is provided under regulations made by the Committee of Lloyd's requiring every underwriter transacting non-marine business to provide each year a cash deposit or a guarantee in a form approved by the Committee of an amount equal to the whole of his premium income for that year derived from his non-marine business.

It will be seen that the regulations under the Act of 1909 also provide for the audit and for the furnishing of a certificate each year to the Committee. This also gives legislative sanction to a practice which had been introduced voluntarily.

Where an underwriter carries on employers' liability insurance within the United Kingdom, the option reserved in regard to fire and accident insurance is not permitted, but the underwriter must make a deposit of £2,000 as provided in the first option above referred to.

The special provisions of the Act of 1909 which relate to Lloyd's were framed to meet the special methods of business as practised at that institution, but their purpose is to ensure as far as reasonably possible that the business is carried on along sound lines.

Chapter 3. LLOYD'S BROKERS

Although the institution of Lloyd's grew out of the association of underwriters, and though even now the members of Lloyd's are practically all underwriters, yet these do not by any means make up the complete personnel working there. In addition to the members, whether they be underwriting members or non-underwriting members, those entitled to use The Room at Lloyd's for the purpose of playing their part in the business transacted there are

Annual Subscribers, who consist mostly of principals and the senior employees of brokerage firms.

Substitutes, who are those employed in a clerical capacity, either by underwriters or by brokers.

Associates, who are persons whose work brings them into touch with members or subscribers, for the purpose of carrying out certain professional services connected with insurance. They include average adjusters, claims assessors, accountants, solicitors, and other professional men.

The British marine-insurance companies, almost without exception, also pay a subscription to Lloyd's in return for which their accredited representatives may enter the Underwriting Room for the purpose of obtaining information and discussing technical matters with Lloyd's underwriters, but they may not transact any insurance business within the Underwriting Room. For their subscription, the marine companies also obtain certain shipping intelligence from Lloyd's.

Of these various classes of persons the brokers form by far the largest part, both numerically and in the importance of their work. As already indicated, the Annual Subscribers are not all brokers, yet every Lloyd's broker must be an Annual Subscriber. The purpose of this chapter is to describe the place of the broker in the work of Lloyd's and to examine how the system is operated. In the first place it must be explained that there is no definite cleavage between members and subscribers, in the sense that a member cannot be a broker or vice versa. Any member, whether underwriting or non-underwriting, is entitled to carry on business also as a broker at Lloyd's, provided that he complies with the rules laid down by the Committee of Lloyd's, and provided also that his business as an underwriter is kept entirely distinct from his business as a broker. Unless, however, a broker happens to be also a member, he has no effective share in the government of Lloyd's; he cannot be elected to the Committee and he has no right to attend or vote at general meetings.

The general purpose of a broker at Lloyd's is to serve as a connecting link between the public who wish to insure and the underwriters who are willing to grant insurance. It must be emphasised that this is the only way in which insurances can be effected at Lloyd's, for the underwriters have no direct connection with their insured, either in arranging the insurance, in issuing the policy, in dealing with claims, or in any other business connection which may arise in relation to the insurance. The broker acts as the intermediary for all purposes, and this is a fundamental feature of the business done at Lloyd's.

There was a time, however, when merchants, shipowners, and in fact almost anybody could go to Lloyd's and do business with the underwriters there. In a lecture to the Insurance Institute of London in 1928, Eric Gibb, himself a broker at Lloyd's, explained that this custom appears to have died down because the inexpert layman generally found the wily underwriter too clever for him and that it paid him better to employ a broker who knew all the tricks of the trade. This must have occurred about the time of the change-over from the status of a coffee house to that of a closed corporation, say about the year 1800. It is obvious from contemporary records that broking as known today was practised during the Angerstein period; in fact Angerstein was himself a broker as well as an underwriter.[1] In those days the status of those entitled to do business at Lloyd's was only vaguely defined, and in view of the rather haphazard development of the Corporation this is not surprising, for the change-over from an informal market centred in the coffee houses, and at Lloyd's Coffee House in particular, to the Corporation as it exists today was really very gradual. So far as broking is concerned, it would seem that the resolution of 2nd April, 1880 (see Chapter 1), was of much significance. Then, it will be remembered, it was decided that "only merchants, bankers, underwriters and insurance brokers should in future be admitted as subscribers," and it may be accepted that thenceforward the haphazard placing of insurances by any who cared to obtain the entry to Lloyd's ceased, and the business settled down into regular channels. It should be

[1] See Chap. 1, p. 15.

noted that even today merchants, bankers, and shipowners are brokers at Lloyd's, not quite in the sense that they were subscribers in the early nineteenth century but rather in the capacity of brokers placing not only their own business but that of clients also. In short these firms are practically water-tight broking concerns associated with the parent firm more or less intimately but carrying on a legitimate broking business as well.

There is no particular form of constitution of a Lloyd's broking firm. It may consist of one person working solely on his own account; it may be a private partnership of two or more persons, with an unlimited liability as is always the case with such partnerships; or it may consist of a private limited company, with the liability of the members limited in accordance with the articles of association. In the case of a one-man business, the owner must, if not already a member, become an Annual Subscriber, and in the case of a partnership, the same must apply to at least one of the partners. Where the firm is a limited company, one of its directors must become a member or Annual Subscriber.

It will be seen that the rule against partnerships among underwriters does not apply to brokers.

Security

Before a firm or a company may become brokers at Lloyd's, certain formalities have to be complied with. A special subscription of £25 per annum, over and above that paid for membership or annual subscribership, must be paid, and in many cases a substantial deposit must be made in approved securities, such securities remaining under the control of the Committee until every liability of the brokerage business

to underwriters has been discharged, but the depositor en-
joys the dividends on his investments so deposited. The
amount of the deposit when required is proportionate to the
volume of business transacted and is fixed by the Committee
of Lloyd's, so no precise figures can be given, but the amount
is substantial and serves as a guarantee of the payment of
premiums due from the depositing broker to the underwriters
with whom he does business.

Legal Position

Since the broker acts as the link between the underwriters
and members of the public wishing to insure, it is important
to consider the legal position of a broker in relation to his
business. It is of the greatest importance to remember that
the broker and the underwriter deal with each other as principals. This means that the broker is not the agent of the underwriter, and in this connection a distinction must be drawn
between business placed by a broker at Lloyd's and business
placed by a broker with an insurance company. In the latter case the broker may be the agent of the insurance company. In actual fact he is always duly appointed as an agent
of the company, though whether in any particular transaction he is acting as agent for the company or as agent for
the proposer must depend upon the circumstances of the
case. Arnould, the author of the leading legal textbook on
marine insurance, expresses the opinion that in certain circumstances the broker may be the agent of both assured and
insurer. The special relationship between brokers and underwriters at Lloyd's is difficult to define, but undoubtedly it
springs from their joint membership in the Corporation. It
is, as it were, the fact that they are members of the same

family which places their relations on a different footing
from that which exists between principal and intermediary
in any other type of business.

In placing business at Lloyd's the broker is the agent of
the proposer and not the agent of the underwriters. This
has certain legal effects on the transaction, for as the broker
is the agent of the proposer any communication which he
makes to the underwriters will be binding on his principal.
Thus should any material fact be wrongly stated by the
broker, that wrong statement will bind the proposer, and
the underwriter might be able to repudiate the contract as
against the proposer. This is a point for the proposer to remember when instructing a broker to place an insurance at
Lloyd's, for if those instructions are wrongly passed on to
the underwriters, the proposer has no remedy except against
the broker. It would be different if the broker were the agent
of the underwriter, for then any knowledge which he possessed as agent would be imputed to the underwriter as
principal, and the underwriter could not then plead that he
had been misinformed. This aspect of the methods of conducting business at Lloyd's emphasises the need for the
most scrupulous care both on the part of a proposer in de-
scribing the nature of the risk to be insured and of the broker
in passing that information on to the underwriter.

The position as stated in the preceding paragraph applies
to the ordinary placing of business in The Room, and there
is of course an exception in those cases where brokers have
been granted binders by the underwriters for the transaction of certain classes of business within certain terms and
conditions. In such cases, the broker holding the binder is
the agent of the underwriter for the purpose to which that

binder relates. Such a broker would obtain his business largely from sub-agents, who are then agents of the insured.

The system in vogue at Lloyd's of dealing only with brokers for the placing of insurances is not a matter of legal precept but arises from the custom and usage of Lloyd's. Nevertheless, the proposer is bound by that usage, for the underwriter is entitled to lay down the terms upon which he is prepared to do business. This usage applies only to the negotiations leading up to the placing of the insurance, and as soon as the contract is completed privity of contract is established between the underwriter and the assured. The name of the assured appears on the policy which is signed by or on behalf of the underwriter. The broker is a pure intermediary and is in no sense a party to the contract. The usage of Lloyd's whereby all matters between the underwriters and the public are dealt with only through brokers is not thereafter legally binding on the assured.

Claims. It has already been stated that not only in arranging the insurance, but also in handling claims or in any other matter relating to the insurance, an underwriter will deal only through a broker. This, however, is only the practice and must be understood as such. It is a practice which is almost always observed, but it cannot be legally enforced against the assured so as to deprive him of any remedies against the underwriter to which he may be entitled under his policy. He may, if he so desires, disregard the usage and insist on dealing direct with the underwriter. This right has been allowed in a number of cases decided in the English courts. Thus in *Dalzell v. Mair* (1808) an assured successfully brought a claim against the underwriter for a return of premium, and in *DeGaminde v. Pigou* (1812) a similar claim for a loss under the policy was allowed. Also in *Macfarlane v. Giannocopulo* (1858) a claim was allowed where the assured had applied without success to the broker for payment. Nevertheless, this is subject to the qualification that the assured may expressly adopt the usage of Lloyd's and authorise the broker to act as his agent in all matters relating to the insurance. Such a course will usually be presumed when an insured is in the habit of dealing with Lloyd's. In that event the broker acts as agent of the assured throughout and any payments made by the underwriter to the broker under the policy are binding on the assured.

Premiums. It is convenient here to explain the position as between underwriter, broker, and assured in regard to the premiums payable under a policy issued at Lloyd's. This is in some respects different from that relating to the payment of claims. In the first place the assured is responsible to the broker for the payment of the premium and only to the broker. The broker may claim payment of the premium even though he may not actually have paid it over to the underwriter. It follows that the underwriter looks to the broker for the payment of the premium to him, and it is immaterial whether the broker has himself actually received the premium from the assured. The usual form of Lloyd's policy contains an acknowledgment that the premium has been paid, the effect of which is that the assured is entitled to enforce the policy against the underwriter even though the premium has not been paid. Nevertheless, the broker would have a lien on the policy for the amount of any unpaid premiums. As between the underwriter and the broker premiums are not paid on individual cases but are dealt with in account at such intervals as may be mutually agreed.

It is important to maintain the distinction between the premium payable by the assured to the broker and by the broker to the underwriter, and any payment which has to be made by the underwriter under the policy. Thus in making good a loss to the assured under the policy, the underwriter is not entitled to deduct any unpaid premium; nor could he refuse to refund a return of premium due to the assured on the ground that the original premium out of which the return had to be made had not been paid to him [*Dalzell v. Mair* (1808)]. If the assured has paid the premium to a broker, who is unable to meet his obligations to the underwriter, so that the underwriter never receives the premium, the assured will have to pay the premium again, because the insolvent broker is his agent. It is clear from what has been said of the position occupied by the broker as between the underwriter and the assured that a great responsibility rests upon him, and he should be a man of substance who can be relied upon to fulfil his obligations.

Placing Insurance

The work carried out by a broker at Lloyd's may best be described by following out in detail the procedure adopted in arranging an insurance.

The Slip. Upon receiving instructions from an intending assured, who for this purpose may be described as the proposer, the broker enters details of the proposal on a sheet of paper of a standard size and shape headed with the name of the firm of brokers and universally known as *the slip*. The use of the slip has the sanction of long-established practice, originating in marine insurance and since extended to non-marine business. The slip plays indeed so important a part in the transaction of business at Lloyd's as to call for a detailed explanation. The particulars entered on the slip must include all the material facts relating to the matter proposed for insurance, so as to set out the proposal in such a way that the underwriter can form a judgment as to the merits of the risk, as to whether he will accept it, and if so at what rate of premium. The manner in which these facts are presented on the slip has become to some extent stereotyped by long usage, especially in marine business, which is carried on today much as it was two hundred years ago. The specimen of a slip (Fig. 1) shows the nature of the information supplied on a marine-insurance slip. The details are given in that particular way because it is familiar to the underwriters and follows a usage to which they have become accustomed. This naturally facilitates their consideration of the risk offered and enables the business to be more expeditiously conducted.

The slip takes the place of a proposal form, and though it is not signed either by the proposer or by the broker acting as his agent, yet the facts disclosed therein are accepted by the underwriter as a true statement and are binding on the proposed insured. If there should be a mistake in some material fact disclosed on the slip, so as to affect the underwriter's judgment, then if the underwriter sought to avoid the policy, the insured could not plead that he was not responsible for the mistake merely because he had not signed the slip, although he might have a right against the broker for neglect in his duty. It would not be convenient for the slip to be put forward as a signed statement of the facts disclosed by the proposer, for as will be seen, that would conflict with

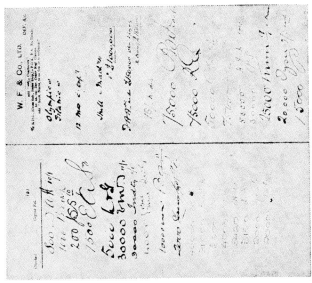

Fig. 1. The "Titanic" slip. (*By courtesy of Messrs. Willis, Faber & Co.,
Ltd.*)

the purpose for which, according to the customs of Lloyd's, the slip is used.

Having prepared his slip, the broker takes it into The Room at Lloyd's and submits it to one or more underwriters, as may be required, each of whom will set down on the slip the amount of the risk which he is prepared to accept on behalf of his Syndicate and affix his initials thereto as evidence thereof.[1] If the rate of premium has not already been agreed upon, he will also add the rate which he proposes to charge. Here it is necessary to remember that when a broker receives instructions from his principal he may be given a "firm order," which means he is to place the risk firm either at an agreed rate of premium or at any rate which the underwriter sees fit to charge; or as is very often the case he may be required merely to obtain a quotation, that is to say, to ascertain whether the underwriters would be willing to write the risk and if so at what rate of premium. The nature of the slip will vary according to the terms of the broker's instructions. In the former case when the firm order has been accepted by the underwriter his initials on the slip have a binding force. In the latter case, although the underwriter may and frequently does initial the slip so as to show the amount he will accept and the rate of premium he requires, yet a binding contract is not thereby established; for the underwriter and the proposed insured are not yet of one mind. The quotation must first be submitted by the broker to his client, who has the right to say whether the terms are acceptable to him. The slip therefore remains for the time being merely a proposal and does not become a cover note

[1] A more detailed description of the procedure is given in Chap. 4.

until the acceptance by the client of the proposed terms has been duly communicated to the underwriter.

The effect of the completed slip is to bind the underwriter to issue a policy in accordance with the particulars submitted. The policy will be in the ordinary terms of a Lloyd's policy, and as these terms are well known to both broker and underwriter it is not necessary to incorporate them in the slip or even to refer to them in any specific way. If, however, there is to be any departure from the terms of the ordinary policy, as by the deletion of any clause, or the incorporation of any new clause, specific reference must be made thereto in the slip. It may be noted that the growth of the non-marine market at Lloyd's has added some importance to this point. There is much greater variation in the nature of the risks submitted for insurance against non-marine risks than is the case in marine insurance. This affects the drafting of the slip both in regard to setting out particulars of the insurance required and also in the inclusion of any special terms to be subsequently incorporated in the policy.

The Marine Slip. It is necessary, and important, to differentiate between the marine and the non-marine slip.

While both represent binding contracts between the parties, the marine slip is not a "legal" contract, in that it cannot be enforced in law or equity. It is true that the Marine Insurance Act lays down in Section 21:

> A contract of marine insurance is deemed to be concluded when the proposal of the assured is accepted by the insurer whether the policy be then issued or not; and for the purpose of showing when the proposal was accepted, reference may be made to the slip or covering note or other customary memorandum of the contract although it be unstamped.

This seems to argue that the slip expresses a legal contract, as indeed it may, but any possibility of enforcing that contract is completely ruled out, so far as the slip is concerned, by Section 22 of the Act which provides that

subject to the provisions of any statute, a contract of marine insurance is inadmissible in evidence unless it is embodied in a marine policy in accordance with this Act. The policy may be executed either at the time when the contract is concluded or afterwards

The Marine Insurance Act is probably the most perfect codification of case law on the English Statute Book, and before going further it is both interesting and important to observe the case law on which this ruling with regard to the slip is based. In the case of *Ionides v. Pacific Fire and Marine Insurance Co.* (1871) Mr. Justice Blackburn said:

The slip is in practice, and according to the understanding of those engaged in marine insurance, the complete and final contract between the Parties, fixing the terms of the insurance and the premium, and neither party can, without the assent of the other, deviate from the terms thus agreed on without breach of faith, for which he would suffer severely in his credit and future business.

The Legislature, for the purpose of protecting the revenue, had by the strongest enactments provided that no such instrument should be given in evidence for any purpose. But all those enactments are repealed by the 30 Vict.c 23 and the law is governed by the 7th and 9th sections of that Act. By section 7 no contract or agreement for sea insurance shall be valid unless expressed in a policy. And by section 9 no policy shall be pleaded or given in evidence in any Court unless duly stamped. As the slip is clearly a contract for marine insurance,

and is equally clearly not a policy, it is, by virtue of these enactments, not valid—that is, not enforceable at law or in
equity; but it may be given in evidence wherever it is, though
not valid, material.

It is true that the Act 30 Vict.c 23—the Act of 1867, which
governed marine insurance at the time of Mr. Justice Blackburn's judgment, has since been superseded by the Marine
Insurance Act 1906 taken in conjunction with certain provisions of the Stamp Act 1891 and amendments thereto, yet the
legal position in regard to this matter remains unaltered. If it
be asked whether a slip might not be converted into a policy
by being stamped, the answer is definitely no, because both
the Marine Insurance Act and the Stamp Act lay down the
essential requirements of a policy, and among these both state
that the policy must state the name or names of the insurers or
underwriters. This in itself would be sufficient to defeat any
attempt to convert a slip into a policy by having it stamped,
since the underwriters' initials, while designating their respective Syndicates, do not constitute the name or names of
the insurers. Further, no policy of insurance, save in very
special circumstances, may be stamped after it has been
signed. It is true that under the Stamp Act a policy of sea
insurance may, for the purpose of production in evidence,
be stamped after it has been executed, subject to a penalty
of £100, but there is no means of enforcing the signature of
underwriters to a policy, and the production of a policy in the
circumstances envisaged in the making of this provision
would require the good will of both parties.

So settled is the law with regard to this point that, while it
has been cited in various cases since the Marine Insurance
Act 1906 was passed, it does not seem to have been ques-

tioned. In view of the very specific provisions of the Act, based, as has been pointed out, on clear-cut case law, any questioning of the situation would seem to be quite hopeless.

Although a claim may occur between the time of initialling the slip and the issue of the policy this need give rise to no real difficulty. In effect the underwriter by initialling the slip has undertaken to issue a policy in accordance therewith. No instance has been known in which any Lloyd's underwriter has attempted to repudiate liability on the grounds that his initial on the slip is not legally binding, and it is inconceivable that any such contingency would ever arise.

If it did, the pressure of public opinion would be so overwhelming that the underwriter would never be shown another risk by any broker, and he would almost certainly bring down upon himself the operation of the machinery which is available for the expulsion of members of Lloyd's from the Corporation.

The Non-marine Slip. In non-marine business the position is different, for in this branch of insurance there is no statutory obligation to issue a policy. Nevertheless, this is always done, if only so that the terms of the contract embodied in the slip may be set out in full detail. Having initialled a non-marine slip the underwriter could not afterwards refuse to issue the policy unless he had grounds for impugning the validity of the slip. There is no particular time limit within which the policy must be put forward for signature, and though there might be unreasonable delay in putting it forward, that would be no excuse for the underwriter to refuse to issue it. Similarly the policy may be and often is issued after a loss has occurred, without in any way affecting the underwriter's liability for that loss. This all goes to show how the insurance contract refers back to the slip, and no delay or omission in the subsequent formalities can affect its validity. It follows that although the effect of the slip is to bind the underwriter to issue a policy this is not its whole effect. It constitutes in itself a binding contract of insurance, and it cannot be objected to on the ground that it does not contain all the terms of the contract, for it must be read in conjunction with the usual form of Lloyd's policy in the class of insurance to which it relates. Moreover, in non-marine insurance it is possible to enforce a claim against the underwriter on the slip alone, if a policy for some reason has not been issued. The legal position was clearly expressed by Mr. Justice Mathew in the case of *Thompson v. Adams* (1889) dealing with a fire-insurance slip in which he said:

> There is no statutory difficulty in the way and no reason why the slip should not be a binding contract and there is every reason for supposing that such would be the intention of the person presenting the slip to be initialled in respect of the risk. . . . I think there was a binding contract to insure and that the contract contained in the slip is not one from which the underwriter could escape on the ground that it was only optional whether or not he should go on with the contract and perfect it by a policy of insurance.

This seems to put the position completely and shows the difference between non-marine insurance and marine insurance, where there would be a statutory difficulty in the way, because the provisions of the Stamp Act 1891 and the Marine Insurance Act 1906 require a stamped policy to be issued in all marine insurances.

Cover Note

The work of the broker does not come to an end with the placing of the insurance. Under the system which has grown up at Lloyd's the broker carries out all the detailed formalities required to bring the matter to completion. In this, the practice is exactly the opposite of that used by insurance companies, for the agent of a company is not concerned with the issue of cover notes or policies. All such detail work is done by the company's staff. When a risk has been placed at Lloyd's, however, the broker's first duty is to issue a *cover note* to his client. A specimen form of cover note is given on page 66. It sets out that an insurance has been effected with Lloyd's underwriters in accordance with the following particulars. These particulars are set out with many recognised abbreviations, but in sufficient detail to make clear what has been insured without specifying the fuller details which will appear on the policy. The terms of the policy are not set out on the cover note though it is a common thing to state that the insurance is as per Lloyd's policy in one or other of its standard forms. At the end of the cover note there is a debit note showing the amount of the premium payable. Sometimes this debit note may not be filled in, as, for example, when cover has been obtained from the underwriters before the amount of the premium has been ascertained. Such a cover note would usually be marked "provisional."

If the order is *open, i.e.,* for a maximum amount which may be reduced, and if there are other details not yet settled, such as the name of the ship in which cargo is to be carried or the date of the commencement of a risk, the cover note

BLANK & CO., Ltd.
      Insurance Brokers

Telephone: SAMple 8331
Telegrams: "Illustrate, London."

EXAMPLE HOUSE,
      15, SPECIMEN STREET,
AND AT LLOYD'S   LONDON, E.C.3   .... 195......

𝔐𝔢𝔪𝔬𝔯𝔞𝔫𝔡𝔲𝔪 𝔬𝔣 𝔓𝔯𝔬𝔳𝔦𝔰𝔦𝔬𝔫𝔞𝔩 𝔍𝔫𝔰𝔲𝔯𝔞𝔫𝔠𝔢 *effected for account of*

.... *as follows:*

.... @ ....

Per ....

Period ....

....

on ....

....

Conditions: ....

....

....

....

....

....

Insured with ....

BLANK & CO., Ltd.

Director.

SPECIMEN FORM OF COVER NOTE

is open also. In the case of open insurances, the broker files
the documents for future use.

Normally a cover note is issued after the terms and conditions of the insurance have been arranged, so that a calculation of the premium to be paid by the insured can be made.
The document then acts as both cover note and premium demand and is commonly called a *debit note*. The insured has

to make payment to the broker of the amount due as soon as he receives the debit note, unless of course he has special arrangements to the contrary. But the amount becomes immediately due and payable by the client, even though the broker may in the ordinary way of business allow time for payment.

The debit note contains not only a statement of the premium due for the insurance and how it is calculated but also a charge for policy and stamp. This charge is retained by the broker, and even though it is usually also shown on the policy, it does not form part of the amount due to the underwriter. The charge falls into two parts, the cost of preparing the policy and the cost of the stamp duty chargeable by law on all insurance policies. As will be seen later the broker has to prepare the policy, so that he must pay for the stamp and also the cost of the policy itself. These costs he recovers from the insured and retains to reimburse himself for his outlay. The charge for stamp duty will be that actually required by law for the particular type of policy; the cost of the policy cannot be so exactly computed. This is composed of cost of paper and printing, clerical labour, and the like, which can be only roughly assessed. There is no universal rule governing the charge for the policy, but this may be 6d. or 1/– for each case according to the circumstances.

The Policy

Following the issue of the cover note the next duty of the broker is to prepare the policy. This again is an invariable rule at Lloyd's. The underwriter never prepares the policy himself, though he may in a specially complicated case agree on the form of wording with the broker before the latter completes the policy. In a normal case the broker selects the printed form of Lloyd's policy appropriate to the risk and fills in the required particulars from the slip, so that the completed document may be put forward for signature.

Records

All the steps in the placing of a risk involve a certain amount of book-keeping. For instance, records must be kept of orders received and of cover notes sent out, and the slip itself is a record of the underwriters who have written the risk. There is no standardised system of book-keeping among Lloyd's brokers. Each office has its own system although the various systems have certain features in common. The policy, when completed by the appropriate signatures, is returned to the broker who then despatches it to his client, and the process of arranging the insurance is finally completed.[1]

In this part of his work the broker again takes up the role of intermediary, not acting as agent for either of the two parties, but bound equally to serve them both. Thus in issuing the cover note to his client, he is at that moment acting on behalf of the underwriters, but he cannot bind them for anything which goes beyond what they have initialled on the slip. If he purports to issue a cover note which is not in fact in accordance with the slip, the insured could not sue the underwriters on the cover note, though he might have a remedy against the broker for breach of duty. Similarly in preparing the policy the broker must see that everything is carried out in accordance with the instructions given to him, so that everything is insured which the proposer had in-

[1] Full details of policy forms and the procedure connected with their completion and of accounting methods are given in Chap. 4.

structed to be insured, and that all the terms and conditions imposed by the underwriters when they initialled the slip are properly inserted. The twofold duty of the intermediary is indicated here, but there are safeguards. The underwriter or Policy Signing Office [1] would not sign the policy unless it was in agreement with the slip, while the insured would return it for amendment if, when he received it, he found it did not correspond with his instructions.

Commissions

It may be readily understood that the duties and responsibilities of a Lloyd's broker call for a considerable measure of professional skill, and he is entitled to a proper remuneration for the services he renders. This is paid by means of a commission on the premiums, allowed to the broker by the underwriter in account. In the first place, therefore, the underwriter pays, even though the broker in placing the insurance is acting on behalf of the insured. But in effect the commission is paid by the insured, because in fixing his rate of premium the underwriter makes allowance for the fact that he will have to allow a certain percentage thereof to the broker for his commission. The rate of commission paid on non-marine business is a matter for arrangement between the underwriter and the broker and depends upon the nature of the insurance placed. In marine business the customary deductions from the premiums are 5 per cent brokerage, and in the case of *cash* accounts, which are accounts settled at the end of each month between the broker and his client, the assured is allowed a *discount* of 10 per cent which is calculated on the gross premium less brokerage. For instance,

[1] For a detailed explanation of the Policy Signing Office, see Chap. 6.

on a premium of £100 the brokerage would be £5 and the
discount would be calculated on £100 — £5 or £95. This
would amount to £9.10.–, which deducted from the gross
premium of £100 would leave the assured to pay the broker
£91.10.–. Since the 1st July, 1935, there has been a general
agreement by which underwriters allow on marine business
a further deduction of 2½ per cent for cargo and ½ per cent
for hull time risks, as additional remuneration to the broker.
Thus, on a cargo risk the premium payable to the underwriter
by the broker would be

	£	s.		
	£100.	–.	–	
Less 5% brokerage	5.	–.	–	
	95.	–.	–	
Less 10% discount	9.	10.	–	
	85.	10.	–	
Less 2½% allowance	2.	2.	9	
	£ 83.	7.	3	net

On hull time business, when very large premiums are involved, payment is frequently made on the deferred basis,
the shipowner paying one-fourth in cash and the balance
in three equal payments of one-fourth payable at 3, 6, and
9 months, under a bankers' guarantee. Where premiums are
paid on this deferred system, the discount allowed to the
assured is 8 per cent.

Access to Lloyd's

Of course a broker or the principals in a broking firm
who are either Underwriting Members, Non-underwriting
Members, or Annual Subscribers, have access to The Room
and may do business there, but they usually employ others
to help in the placing of risks and other work at Lloyd's.

Such assistants will be either Annual Subscribers or Substitutes. Senior members of a broker's staff who are not principals, but who may be transacting a considerable amount of their own business on a *half brokerage* basis, are often Annual Subscribers, thereby gaining a status in the community which places them on a rather higher plane than that of the Substitutes who are, in fact, clerks authorised to enter The Room and to do business therein on behalf of their employers. They take their title from the fact that they are substitutes for the member or Annual Subscriber who employs them. In recent years, up to the end of 1939, the employer paid £10.0.0 per annum for each Substitute, but by 1940 the fee was increased to £15.0.0. Another class of employee has the right to enter The Room but must not do business there. They are office messengers who carry slips, orders, and messages in general between the brokers' offices and those working in The Room, and they are colloquially known as "White Ticket" boys, being given white cardboard tickets which must be shown to any waiter who challenges them.

The third class of those who have the right to enter The Room at Lloyd's are Associates. These are men who are engaged in business other than that of marine or non-marine insurance, but who may require the right of entry to Lloyd's in order to carry out their business, whatever it may be. Amongst these Associates are chartered accountants, average adjusters, non-marine claims assessors, solicitors who specialise in insurance legal work, and sometimes bank managers. Both average adjusters and non-marine claims assessors must have every opportunity of consulting with underwriters, while a solicitor engaged on important legal work in connection with insurance may also find it necessary to consult with his clients without the delay or inconvenience of having to "call" them to the barrier. Incidentally, all these different classes of those with the right of entry to Lloyd's, with the exception of the White Ticket boys, enjoy the amenities of Lloyd's, such as the right to lunch in the Captains' Room and to use the Reference Room where the principal English newspapers, a wide range of technical publications, and many works of reference, such as city and county directories, trade annuals, and social references, are available. Strictly speaking, the Library, which leads off the Underwriting Room, is for the use only of members, underwriting or non-underwriting, but by an unwritten but freely observed law, those who have the right of entry to Lloyd's may use the Library to consult any book or other reference in it that is not otherwise available. The use of the Library for writing letters and for work which takes more than a brief visit to look up a reference is, however, confined to members only.

It should be understood that The Room at Lloyd's is strictly private and is reserved solely for the use of those entitled to work there. No member of the general public may enter The Room itself, though he may go to the barrier which stands at the entrance to The Room within the precincts of Lloyd's Building, and by application to the waiter in attendance may call by name any person whom he desires to see. The call is made by the Crier who sits in the rostrum erected in the centre of The Room, above which hangs the Lutine Bell. In practice calls go on almost without cessation the whole day, and it is a matter of surprise to the uninitiated that amid the noise and bustle of a normal day in The Room it is possible for underwriters or brokers to hear their names called, and yet they almost invariably do.

Chapter 4. THE BUSINESS DONE
AT LLOYD'S

The purpose of this chapter is to describe the business done at Lloyd's and to explain the contractual relations established when risks are insured. It is not intended to deal with the basic principles of the classes of insurance transacted for that would be much too wide a subject for the compass of this book. These principles are adequately dealt with in the textbooks on the various classes of insurance. Reference to them will be made here only so far as may be necessary to make plain the business carried on at Lloyd's.

Insurance business as transacted at Lloyd's is divided into two classes, marine and non-marine, the latter being a comprehensive term embracing a small volume of short-term life assurance and all other kinds of insurance other than marine. This is a distinction not met with in any other insurance centre, and it arises from the fact that the original purpose of Lloyd's was to promote the transaction of marine insurance and nothing else. Indeed the business was confined to marine for the first two hundred years of the existence of Lloyd's except for certain contingency risks, such as insurances on the life of Napoleon and the like, but to extend it in a general way to any other class of insurance would at one time have been considered quite impossible. Non-marine business was undertaken at first on quite modest lines by underwriters of initiative and enterprise who, we may suppose, saw opportunities for business outside the time-honoured circle of marine insurance and had sufficient courage to venture into the unknown. Marine business had been practised since about 1680, but it was not until 1882 that the first non-marine policy was issued. That was a fire policy. In 1889 the first burglary insurance at Lloyd's was granted, and in 1895 an insurance was first made on earthquake risk. As mentioned in Chapter 1, Lloyd's Act 1871, by which the Society was constituted in its modern form, restricted its objects to the carrying on of marine insurance by its members. The early ventures into the non-marine business were outside the Act, and the position was not regularised until the passing of Lloyd's Act 1911 by which the objects were extended to the carrying on by members of insurance of every description. Since then many new kinds of insurance have been added to the non-marine activities, including "all risks," personal accident, and in comparatively recent times, the important sections motor and aviation, together with many miscellaneous risks.

The Marine-insurance Market

Although the marine business transacted at Lloyd's constitutes a substantial part of the whole, the marine-insurance market in England extends over a wider scope, and a brief description of it may help to clarify the position. The market as a whole is composed partly of Lloyd's Underwriters, partly of marine-insurance companies, and partly of certain underwriting syndicates in Glasgow. These last operate on the same principles as those in force at Lloyd's and are the only syndicates of names now carrying on business in that way outside Lloyd's. Marine insurance had been practised in

England in some form many years before the establishment of Lloyd's Coffee House, and one of the early references to the business is found in an Act of Queen Elizabeth passed in 1601. The early records of the business are very incomplete, and much of what was done can only be conjectured, but it seems certain that, at first, marine risks were accepted only by individual underwriters. The first marine-insurance companies were established in 1720, when the Royal Exchange Assurance and the London Assurance were incorporated by Royal Charter. These two ancient corporations had a monopoly in the sense that no other insurance companies were permitted to transact marine business. This continued for just over a century until the passing of the Marine Insurance Act 1824, so that up to that time the English market was shared by the two corporations mentioned and various individual underwriters or syndicates at Lloyd's, in Liverpool and Glasgow, and elsewhere.

The abolition of the company monopoly in 1824 led to the formation of various new companies, though the process was not very rapid. The first of the postmonopoly companies, both founded in 1824, were the Alliance Marine and General and the Indemnity Mutual. These companies were soundly constructed and have continued in existence up to the present day. During the next 10 years several other companies were formed some of which continued for a time, but all eventually passed away. The next substantial company was founded in 1836. This was the Marine Insurance Co. Ltd., which is still in being. Thereafter the development of the marine-company market slowed up for a time, though there was a short-lived boom in 1845, following the passing of the Joint Stock Registration Act in 1844. Thirteen new companies were formed in that year, but only one survived for as long as 3 years, and some of the ventures of that time were not entirely free from reproach. The Ocean Marine established in 1859 was the only company of that period which was able to make good.

It needed some outside event to act as a stimulus to the growth of marine companies. This was supplied by the American Civil War (1860–1865) which brought an inevitable boom in marine insurance. During that period many of the present-day marine companies were formed, including the London and Provincial, the Thames and Mersey, the Commercial Union, the British & Foreign, the Union Marine, the Maritime, the Merchants' Marine, and the Standard Marine. While some of these were entirely new ventures, some of them represented the establishment as joint-stock companies of businesses previously carried on by syndicates of individual underwriters, especially some of the companies formed in Liverpool. It is perhaps reasonable to say that the effect of this period in the evolution of the marine-insurance market was that the company had become recognised as the unit of marine insurance. This involved the gradual disappearance of the individual underwriter except at Lloyd's where the system is a fundamental part of the organisation.

The close of the American Civil War in 1865 marked the end of the first period of development after the abolition of the monopoly in 1824. The next period continued up to the end of the nineteenth century and was characterised by alternate boom and depression. A number of companies came into the market when business was good. This set up a state of severe competition which reduced the possibility of profitable underwriting. A lean period followed which had the effect of driving from the market all but those concerns which were founded on a solid basis and conducted their affairs in a careful manner. Then followed the developments of the present century, with a period of severe losses in the early years leading to a recovery which culminated in 1913. There followed First World War, 1914–1918, with its enormous increase in business both marine and war. Many new concerns were floated, some on the flimsiest foundation and controlled by inexperienced staffs. A subsequent slump was inevitable, and though conditions made this a gradual process the reaction when it came was the more severe, and from 1920 onwards the number of failures and retirements from the business was unprecedented. The First World War, however, left one indelible mark on the market. It brought into marine business a number of old and well-established companies previously engaged only in non-marine business. These offered unquestioned security and were able to obtain a large share of the business.

At the same time another process was going on, the amalgamation of companies into large groups, with a powerful company at the head, which obtained control of others by absorption, or amalgamation, or acquisition of shares. This process affected all the independent marine companies which passed into one or other of these groups, with one exception, The Sea Insurance Co. of Liverpool, today the only marine-insurance company retaining its absolute independence. The present marine-company market in Great Britain comprises about seventy-five joint-stock concerns, transacting marine business either alone or in conjunction with other classes of insurance through their marine departments.

The marine-insurance companies are located in London and in Liverpool with branches in a few of the principal ports

such as Hull, Manchester, and Glasgow. The great majority of
the companies have their head offices in London and are members of the Institute of London Underwriters. The Liverpool
marine companies arose mostly out of private syndicates
which used to operate in the underwriting rooms at Liverpool, a development which began about 1850, when joint
stock concerns were coming into vogue, but marine insurance
had long been practised in Liverpool, and the Liverpool Underwriters' Association, founded in 1802, is the oldest institution of its kind in England. The Institute of London Underwriters is of more recent formation and was established in
1884. It originated from informal meetings of marine-
company secretaries and claims adjusters who had formed
the habit of resorting to the Jamaica Wine House in Cornhill
to discuss in a quite informal way matters of common interest
relating to their business. The Institute of London Underwriters is now the leading institution of its kind in the English market, and though it does not function as a complete
tariff organisation in the sense in which that term is understood in other branches of insurance, it is the recognised authority for drafting special policy clauses and for promoting
agreements between its members.

In so far as market agreements and the drafting of clauses
are concerned, the Institute operates in close collaboration
with Lloyd's Underwriters' Association. For instance, the
Joint Hull Committee, the Technical and Clauses Committee,
the War Risk Rating Committee, and the Joint Cargo Committee, while mainly administered by the Institute, are constituted of members from both companies and Lloyd's Underwriters. At the weekly meeting of claims adjusters Lloyd's
claims adjusters participate equally with those of the com-

panies, and the Chairman and Deputy Chairman are elected
one from each component of the market. The Institute does
not, however, promote a schedule of tariff ratings, except
in regard to war-risk insurances and except that it imposes
scales of additional premiums for condoning breaches of
Institute warranties and introduced also during the Second
World War a scale of "surcharges" to offset the increased
maritime perils of wartime navigation which charges have
since been continued.

The last component part of the marine-insurance market
in England is made up of the underwriters transacting that
class of business at Lloyd's. Although the company market
and the Lloyd's market are distinct from one another there is
much co-operation between them. It will be remembered that
all the marine companies are Annual Subscribers to Lloyd's
and have the right of entry to The Room. Also the Institute of
London Underwriters works in close association with Lloyd's
marine underwriters on matters of principle. For this purpose a number of joint committees mentioned above have
been set up, such as the Joint Hull Committee, the Technical
and Clauses Committee, and the Joint Cargo Committee
which are permanent committees with well-defined powers.
In addition, from 1935 to 1940, there was the Joint War Risk
Rating Committee which still exists. The marine underwriters
at Lloyd's have their own association known as Lloyd's Underwriters' Association, established in 1909. It does not bear
the distinguishing name Marine, because at that time this
was the only class of business which Lloyd's was empowered
to transact under its Acts. But marine is the only class of business this Association deals with, and to some extent it serves
the same purpose towards Lloyd's Underwriters as the In-

stitute of London Underwriters does towards the companies. Its activities, however, are more domestic and concerned with the private business interests of its members. Thus it promotes agreements between its members but it issues no policy clauses of its own, though it takes its share in the drafting of clauses through its membership of the joint committees of the Institute of London Underwriters. It should be noted that the clauses published in a booklet by Witherby & Co. and known as Lloyd's Clauses refer only to fire and other nonmarine business, though there are a few marine clauses in use, which are colloquially called Lloyd's Clauses, as, for example, the Janson Clause which was drafted by an underwriter of that name.

Other associations of a similar kind exist in Lloyd's nonmarine market. Lloyd's Underwriters' Fire and Non-Marine Association was established in 1910, one year before the passing of the Lloyd's Act which regularised the transaction of non-marine business. This association looks after the common interests of those underwriters who belong to it, but exercises rather wider powers than its counterpart in the marine market. It has approved the wording of a number of policy forms and special policy clauses and is also responsible for the survey organisation which has been set up to work in certain classes of non-marine business and which carries out surveys on behalf of the members of the association. To meet the growth of other classes of insurance Lloyd's Motor Underwriters' Association has been set up to deal with motor insurance, and Lloyd's Aviation Underwriters' Association to deal with aviation insurance. It may be stressed that all these underwriters' associations are entirely distinct from the Corporation of Lloyd's. They work in close harmony with the Corporation and would do nothing to transgress any of the laws—written or unwritten—by which Lloyd's is governed. But they are essentially organisations of the underwriting members, whose interests they serve; they hold their own funds and are governed by their own officers on a basis quite separate from the Corporation.

Although the marine and non-marine markets at Lloyd's are distinct from one another, there is no very definite line of cleavage. It is true that the majority of underwriting Syndicates are engaged in either marine or non-marine, yet there are a few Syndicates engaged in both, and there is nothing in the rules of Lloyd's to debar them. The separation of Syndicates into marine and non-marine is due mainly to the technical nature of the business, for the underwriter who is skilled in the practice of marine insurance would not be acquainted with the intricacies of non-marine insurance, while the converse is equally true. Those few Syndicates which transact both marine and non-marine require the services of technical experts in both branches. The marine market dealing with only one class of insurance is the simpler of the two and follows, in its methods, the rules by which marine insurance has developed over the past few centuries.

Non-marine business as carried on at Lloyd's is much more diverse in character including as it does all branches except marine. Thus it embraces such well-known lines of insurance as fire, burglary, motor, third-party, personal-accident and sickness, and many other smaller branches. Many kinds of insurance which today are well known were originated at Lloyd's, such as loss-of-profits insurance, weather insurance, and the like. A great pioneer in the development of these new branches was the late Cuthbert E. Heath, who by enter-

prise and initiative was largely responsible for the growth
of the non-marine market at Lloyd's. The more flexible organisation of Lloyd's made it easier for new branches of
insurance to be tried than was possible in the more rigid
company world, and though it is not strictly true to say
that any risk can be insured at Lloyd's—for the underwriters
are sound businessmen who would not assume risks which
were by their nature not fit subjects for insurance—yet the
facilities available in the non-marine market do undoubtedly
provide for a very wide range of risks and many different kinds of hazard. So great has been the development
of this side of the business that for some years before 1939
the premium income derived from the non-marine business exceeded that derived from the marine business, in
spite of the latter's two centuries' start. This is not necessarily
permanent, for it depends on the run of the business at any
given time.

Placing a Risk

The working of the insurance markets at Lloyd's may be
illustrated by reference to what is done in the placing of a
risk. First we may deal with the arrangements of a marine insurance. Suppose that a grain shipper has instructed his
Lloyd's broker to cover a particular shipment of grain from
Buenos Aires to Liverpool by the steamer *Portlight* sailing
on or about a stated date. On receipt of the order the broker
makes out a slip for submission to the underwriters.[1] In the
practice of the marine market, there are two kinds of slip,
plain slips and *special* slips. The plain slip is in blank with

[1] The nature and purpose of the slip have already been explained
(see Chap. 3).

only the name of the broker at the top; the special slip has printed on it in addition the abbreviated details of the conditions applicable to some of the more common risks offered for insurance. For the purpose of the present illustration it may be assumed that a plain slip is used. The broker enters on the slip the details of his order, including the name of the steamer, the voyage, the interest to be insured, the proposed policy conditions, and possibly the rate of premium at which he hopes to place the business. There is no hard-and-fast rule or formula for making out slips. Each broker has his own method though broadly speaking they all follow established practice and are alike in that they give the details necessary to inform the underwriters of what is to be insured and to enable them to make a proper assessment of the risk.

When the slip has been prepared the broker takes it into The Room at Lloyd's and goes to the Box of the underwriter whom he considers suitable for the purpose of insuring the risk. In selecting the underwriter he has certain considerations in mind: who is likely to quote him a reasonable rate of premium; who will write a substantial part of the risk; and, what is most important, whose name is a good lead. It is seldom that a risk is insured entirely with one underwriter. It is usual for each to accept only a share, perhaps quite a small share, according to the circumstances. It is an outstanding feature of the methods of business at Lloyd's that an underwriter builds up his business in the main by accepting a very large number of risks but for a small share only of each, thereby securing for himself the utmost protection of the law of average. It will therefore be necessary for the broker to approach a number of underwriters with his slip before he can complete the insurance, and each underwriter will write

on the slip the amount he is prepared to accept. The underwriter whose name appears first on the slip is *the lead,* and
the question of the lead is one of the most important factors
in insurance at Lloyd's, since it exercises a considerable influence on those underwriters who follow on the slip. The
broker must therefore use discrimination in choosing the
underwriter whom he wishes to lead. In the case now being
considered he would seek an underwriter known to be an expert in grain insurance and perhaps in South American grain
insurance in particular. When the succeeding underwriters
see at the head of the slip the name of an acknowledged expert in the type of business in question, they will accept the
fact that he has written it as at least some guarantee that
it is a good risk and written on satisfactory terms and conditions. This will make them the more ready to accept a share
themselves and will facilitate the work of the broker in placing the full insurance. In the days of John Julius Angerstein
(see Chapter 1) it was said that his prestige was so high that
if he was the first underwriter on the slip the broker was
certain of completing his order without further trouble.
Such risks were colloquially known in the market as "Julians."

The underwriter holding the lead will generally accept a
substantial share of the risk, and it is desirable for the broker
that he should do so. If he wrote but a small part it would
look as if he had not much faith in it, and the following underwriters would be influenced accordingly. The selection of
the right lead calls for a nice judgment on the part of the
broker, though of course a broker with a long and wide experience finds this a comparatively easy task because he becomes thoroughly acquainted with his market.

Every Lloyd's broker has access to the whole of the available market and may offer his business to any underwriter he chooses, although it would be useless to offer a class of risk to an underwriter who was known not to write that particular class. It is a common misapprehension in some quarters that certain brokers deal only with certain groups of underwriters, while other brokers deal with other underwriters. Quite frequently, when a broker has been unable to place a risk, the proposer will approach another broker to know if he can place it with his underwriters, under the mistaken idea that the first broker had not access to the whole of the underwriters available. This is quite wrong, for every Lloyd's broker is fully acquainted with the whole of the market, and if one broker fails to place a risk it will not be because there are some underwriters whom he cannot or does not approach. This is not to say that because one broker has been unable to place an insurance no other broker could possibly succeed in doing so, for there are often reasons why one broker may be successful where another has failed, through special influence with underwriters, or a more specialised knowledge of the market, and so on.

Having shown the slip to the underwriter whom he wishes to lead the risk, the broker may add a few words of explanation, or he may place the slip before the underwriter without comment, leaving the latter to ask his own questions. There is no particular technique in use for showing risks at Lloyd's; each broker has his own, though a plain straightforward manner of dealing with his business will always stand a broker in good stead and incline the underwriter to listen to him and to give him a sympathetic hearing.

The Lloyd's system of transacting business is a very democratic one. In dealings between underwriter and broker,

"first come first served" is the rule. This is important in the
case of a busy underwriter occupying a leading position in
one of the larger markets. At some of the underwriters'
boxes, so many brokers may desire to show business at the
same time that it is necessary for them to await their turn in
a queue, and it is a point of honour that the broker next in
turn to do business will not listen to the conversation or in
any way attempt to learn the nature of the business which
is being discussed between the underwriter and the broker
at the head of the queue. Seeing that the broker next in turn
is only a few inches away, this involves a certain amount of
tact, but the unwritten law against eavesdropping is strictly
upheld, even though at times it is impossible to avoid over-
hearing words spoken in ordinary tones. The queue itself is
regulated strictly, and the right of the broker to his place
therein is inviolable. A very important broker with a large
risk to place may be waiting behind a junior clerk with some
quite unimportant matter to attend to, but the junior has
the right of way, and the important broker must await his
turn. Any attempt to thrust himself forward would be met
by a request from the underwriter to take his place in the
queue.

In offering his risk for insurance, the broker may not always find his way quite smooth. The first underwriter to
whom he shows it may not be willing to write it, and it may
be necessary for the broker to go on from one underwriter
to another until he has obtained the lead he requires. Thereafter he must continue to show the slip to other underwriters
until he has covered the full amount of his order, and if the
risk is a very large one he may have to visit every underwriter
with whom he does business of that class. It may often be

necessary to show the business also to some of the insurance companies, and in the marine department this is frequently done. The process is the same whether the underwriter be at Lloyd's or in the service of a company.

This method of writing risks is traditional and is perhaps the most simple commercial practice known. The underwriter inscribes on the slip the amount he is willing to underwrite and appends his initials, the initials being the custom of the business and sufficient to bind the underwriter even though this may be regarded as somewhat informal. The underwriter's initials soon become as well known as the full name, and instantly convey to the mind of the broker the underwriting Syndicate represented. The initials used by an underwriter are not necessarily his own; they may be those of the first name in the Syndicate or those of an underwriter member of the Syndicate who has long since passed away. As an example, a well-known underwriter, Sir Eustace Pulbrook (who was chairman of Lloyd's in 1926 and again from 1940 to 1946 and in 1948) uses the initials "J.L.W." which are those of James Leverton Wylie, an underwriter of the early nineteenth century who wrote for the Syndicate for which Sir Eustace Pulbrook is now the underwriter. The Names constituting that Syndicate have changed many times during the one hundred years and more of its existence, but its identity remains unchanged, and the initials used denote that Syndicate to all who have business with it.

After placing his initial on the slip and the amount he is willing to underwrite (his *line*) the underwriter adds his *Bureau Number*. Since the institution of *Lloyd's Policy Signing Office*—sometimes called Lloyd's Bureau—every syndicate at Lloyd's has been allotted a number for convenience of identification, and this number is always added after the initials.[1]

The method of dealing with business in the marine market has been described by reference to the placing of a single risk which the broker has taken round the market from one underwriter to another until he has completed it. In practice no broker would work in that way, unless business was particularly slack. Each day he has a number of orders, some new ones coming in by that morning's mail, others left over incompleted from previous days. He takes all these slips with him, usually in an oblong leather case specially made for the purpose, and he will show to each underwriter whom he visits such of the slips as he thinks he may be able to place with that underwriter. Large broking firms may often employ a number of substitutes to offer their business, and in many cases each may have his own special department, so that one may deal with hull risks, another with cargo risks, another with reinsurances, and another with non-marine business, or as the case may be. Each specialist broker becomes thoroughly conversant with the technicalities of his own section of the business and is the better able to place risks before the underwriters for consideration and to bring out the salient features. This is also an advantage to the underwriter and improves the service which the broking firm is able to render to its clients.

In the non-marine market the methods used closely resemble those already described for the marine market. The fact that there is a much greater diversity of risk leads to a greater degree of specialisation by the underwriters engaged

[1] The functions of Lloyd's Policy Signing Office are explained on a later page.

in this market. Thus one Syndicate may specialise in employers'-liability business, another in motor business, another in fire and burglary business, and so on. Some amount of specialisation is a help to the underwriters in non-marine business, in that it adds to their experience of the class in which they are engaged and spreads their business over a reasonably wide scope. It also assists the brokers because they know what Syndicates to approach with any given class of risk. In the placing of risks, however, there is no difference in the procedure from that applying to the marine market, though possibly the risks in the non-marine market are more often such that one underwriter can accept the whole, or at least that fewer underwriters are required to complete the insurance than might be necessary in marine business. This has some effect in reducing the work of the broker.

In fire and burglary business it is often necessary for risks to be surveyed, which is done through Lloyd's Underwriters' Fire and Non-Marine Association. In that case the underwriter, though he may agree to hold the risk covered, will delay his final acceptance on the slip until he has had an opportunity to peruse the survey report.

Reinsurance

An important part of the non-marine market is the reinsurance business which is freely transacted therein. Reinsurance by one Syndicate with another is a common feature of the business at Lloyd's, in both the marine and non-marine markets, this being the ordinary prudent practice whereby an underwriter reduces his liabilities when these appear to have become too heavy. The reinsurance business transacted in the non-marine market is of a different kind. It comes princi-

pally from outside Lloyd's and is derived from other insurance organisations in all parts of the world. This reinsurance
business is largely arranged under treaty contracts, but there
is also a considerable volume of facultative reinsurance transacted. The business is done in all branches of the non-marine
market and forms part of the aggregate business accepted
by the underwriters. The reinsurance is partly on a sharing
basis ceded under surplus treaties, and partly on an excess-of-
loss basis. By the sharing or surplus method the underwriter
accepts a proportionate share of the risk ceded at a like
share of the original premium. By the excess-of-loss method
the underwriters are liable only for the amount by which
any one claim exceeds an agreed figure and receive an agreed
percentage of the original premium. Lloyd's underwriters
were the pioneers in this method of reinsurance, which has
grown to great proportions in modern practice.

Life Assurance

Although the non-marine market deals almost entirely
with those classes of insurance ordinarily written in the fire
and accident departments, there is also a small volume of
short-term life assurance written in this market by one Syndicate. This is of a special type, however. The ordinary life-
assurance contract of a permanent nature extending over a
definite period of years or over the whole life of the assured
would not be suitable for an insurance institution such as
Lloyd's. For one reason, owing to death or resignations, the
personnel of Lloyd's Syndicates must change from time to
time; the liability of each member of the Syndicate being
individual, such Syndicates can enter into contracts only for
definite and comparatively short periods and not for in-

definite or long periods. The life business written at Lloyd's takes this point into account, and policies are issued only to secure payment of a certain sum in the event of the assured's dying within the year of assurance. Such policies may be renewed, however, but only on a short-term basis.

Foreign Business

An important part of the business transacted at Lloyd's is derived from foreign sources, and there can be little doubt that this has increased greatly in volume during recent years. It is of interest to reflect how the scope of Lloyd's business has developed throughout the years. In its earliest years Lloyd's dealt only with the London market, and its extension to other parts of the British Isles must have been gradual and as the demand arose. The primary purpose of Lloyd's was without doubt to insure risks originating in its own country. Those risks were of course for many years marine risks only, originating in England but operating all over the world, and this aspect of the business would familiarise the underwriters with foreign business, for in one sense their business has always been on a world-wide basis. It would be a simple step to extend the underwriting operations so as to accept business originating in foreign countries, or risks situate exclusively in those countries and for the interest of foreign nationals. It is not possible to say when this was first begun, but it may be that the development of the non-marine branch played a significant part in stimulating the growth of the foreign business. This business is transacted both direct and by way of reinsurance.

The method of transacting foreign business is the same as that used for home business. Every risk, no matter what its

nature or where it comes from, must be offered by a Lloyd's
broker. Lloyd's Underwriters have no system of foreign
branches and agencies such as that used by insurance companies; every risk must be dealt with in The Room individually between the underwriter and the broker.

Sub-agents. Some of the larger firms of Lloyd's brokers
have set up branch offices in foreign countries, or what is
perhaps more usual have appointed as sub-agents a number of broking firms in various parts of the world. Such
branches or sub-agents would send to their principals in
London particulars of risks which it is desired to place at
Lloyd's, and the principals would do what was necessary to
arrange the insurance. In some cases the branch or sub-agent
is given a certain defined power to bind the principal. In
that case the agent in the foreign country could himself grant
cover to a client, for the class of insurance and up to the
amount on any one risk which had been agreed in the arrangement between the agent and principal. An arrangement
such as this is a *broker's cover*, which always defines exactly
what class of insurance may be covered and the limit up to
which the agent may insure. The principal in London must
of course make the necessary arrangements with underwriters
at Lloyd's to grant the required protection in respect of
these risks. The sub-agent may be acting for the broker, but
it is the underwriter, not the broker, who assumes liability
for the insurances required. In no circumstances may a broker,
as broker, be himself responsible for the risks insured, and
the meaning of the term broker's cover must be understood
accordingly. An example of such a cover might be where a
Lloyd's broker had a big connection in, say, Spain, with a
number of sub-agents connected with the wine trade. He

would then take out a world-wide marine cover with one or
more Syndicates at Lloyd's on wine shipped from Spain.
This would enable him to advise his agents in Spain of the
rates of premium for any particular voyage and they could
issue binding cover or other similar contract to their clients
without specific reference to their principals. Any interest
so insured would be periodically declared under the cover
which the broker had obtained at Lloyd's. A Lloyd's policy
would be issued in respect of the cover granted in the name
of the broker with the addition of the words "and/or as
agent." The policy is issued in the broker's name to save the
trouble and expense of issuing separate policies for every
declaration made under the cover, and the words added are
to show that the broker is covered not for his own interests
but as agent for other people. The broker, being the insured
named in the policy, would be entitled to make a claim thereunder but would have to hold any amounts so recovered
as agent for the persons ultimately entitled thereto. A single policy of this nature would be issued only where the cover
refers to risks of the same class although for different interests. Where authority is granted to a sub-agent to bind his
principal over the whole range of fire insurance, for example, covering risks of many different kinds, it would be usual
to issue separate Lloyd's policies for each different insured, in
the name of the insured and not of the Lloyd's broker.

It is quite usual for a sub-agent in a foreign country to
be granted authority by his principal in London to issue
cover binding on underwriters at Lloyd's, subject to certain
provisions contained in the agreement between the principal and sub-agent. There would always be a definite sum
fixed on any one risk beyond which the sub-agent could not

go; this would correspond with the extent of the cover which the principal had obtained from the underwriters. The class of insurance which may be covered is specified, for example, fire or motor or personal accident or as the case may be, and often the types of risk permitted to be covered are strictly defined, or else there will be a list of risks which may not be accepted. This arrangement is rather wider than that commonly known as a broker's cover because it applies to all kinds of interests, and premium rates may have to be quoted for each risk even though the sub-agent is authorised to issue cover. Policies are issued for each risk in the name of the insured and not in the name of the broker. In these respects the arrangement works in the same way as if the business originated in London; it merely provides a means to facilitate the smooth working of the business, having regard to the fact that the risk to be covered is situate in a foreign country far removed from the Underwriting Room at Lloyd's in London where it is to be insured.

Foreign Laws. In considering the scope of the foreign business transacted at Lloyd's, some attention must be devoted to the question of the laws of different countries. It is well known that many countries have laws in force placing restrictions on the transaction of direct insurance by foreign insurers. This may be done either by prohibiting such insurance altogether—though this is rare—or by imposing certain conditions on foreign insurers under which alone they may transact business in the country. This kind of discriminating legislation has developed considerably in recent years and reflects the growth of the nationalistic spirit since the conclusion of the First World War. The provisions governing the admission of foreign insurers to do business in a country differ as between various nations, being more severe in some cases than in others, but they mostly have two things in common; they provide for a deposit to be made with the government of the country before a license to transact business will be granted, and they require a periodical statement of affairs to be lodged, say once a year, in a prescribed form. The purpose of the deposit is to ensure that an insurer shall prove itself to be of substance and able to allocate funds which shall provide some measure of security for the policyholders in the country. It is a condition of the deposit that if the insurer ceases to do business in the country no part of the deposit will be released until all liabilities incurred in the country have been entirely extinguished. The purpose of the annual statement of accounts is to enable a watch to be kept on the progress of the insurer's business so that the authorities may be satisfied that the insurer is conducting its business on a sound financial basis. Without going into too much detail in this matter it is true to say that today it is the rule that a foreign insurer must be admitted or licensed to do business, before he can properly transact insurance in a country other than his own.

It is not perhaps altogether surprising that as Lloyd's developed their foreign business difficulties arose in complying with the laws relating to admission—difficulties which indeed have been well known in the American market. The position of Lloyd's is quite different from that of an insurance company. A company wishing to open up for business abroad must appoint a branch manager or general agent and set up some kind of an organisation in the country concerned. It becomes at once subject to the laws of the country and cannot commence to operate through this organisation until the laws have been complied with. A Lloyd's underwriter is in no such position. He conducts his business in one place only—the Underwriting Room in London; he has no agents either at home or abroad; the Lloyd's broker in London is not his agent, and still less is the sub-agent of the broker obtaining foreign risks for insurance, except in so far as either of them may hold authority from the underwriter under a binder. The underwriter does not form a definite plan to open up for business abroad. The broker may do that certainly but never the underwriter. The business comes to him at his Box in London; he does not advertise or canvass for business; he simply responds to a demand made upon him by those with business to place. The fact that for many years past business has gone to Lloyd's from countries in which they were not admitted to do the business has undoubtedly given rise to much controversy, but in fairness to the underwriters, the special position in which they are placed and the way their business comes to them ought not to be forgotten.

However, in course of time the underwriters at Lloyd's have come to recognise the difficulties which exist, and something has been done to ease the situation. Let us be clear on this. The Corporation of Lloyd's cannot comply with the laws of other countries in this matter, for in its corporate capacity Lloyd's can do no business falling within the scope of those laws. Such arrangements as can be made must be negotiated with individual Syndicates or perhaps groups of Syndicates accepting business from the country in question. Arrangements have accordingly been made by which groups of Lloyd's Underwriters have agreed to comply with regulations as far as it may be possible for them to do so, as, for example, by making agreed deposits with the state, or by appointing a responsible agent to represent them for legal purposes. This was done, for instance, following recent legislation regulating the conduct of insurance business in France. It is not usually possible, however, for underwriters at Lloyd's to comply with the laws to the full extent possible to companies, and in Norway, for example, the laws were modified so as to make it possible to afford recognition to Lloyd's Underwriters. It is usual to find a spirit of mutual co-operation in such negotiations, which perhaps is to be expected. Each side has something to gain. The underwriters are glad to have their business regularised by the authorities, while the authorities for their part obtain at least some control over business which it is admitted could not be prevented from going to Lloyd's in any event, except possibly by severe penal legislation.

Security. In the United States it has for many years been a sore point that business should be done with Lloyd's Underwriters, while they were not admitted insurers as required by the law, but something has been done to minimise this feeling. In the state of Illinois, for example, legislation has been passed whereby Lloyd's Underwriters can operate legally in that state subject to certain deposits being made with the state authorities. Provided these deposits are earmarked for the purposes intended, *i.e.*, to provide security for the fulfilment of the Underwriters' obligations, it does not matter who makes them. Another important step to smooth out difficulties was taken shortly before the outbreak of the Second World War in September, 1939, by the setting up of Lloyd's American Trust Fund.[1] In addition to the security furnished

[1] See Chap. 7.

by these deposits, Lloyd's Underwriters have also set up certain foreign-currency balances but only in United States dollars and Canadian dollars. Originally the business done at Lloyd's was transacted exclusively in sterling, premiums being received and claims paid in that currency only. This system obtains almost entirely today, and Lloyd's Underwriters do not follow the custom commonly adopted by insurance companies of setting up currency balances in all the countries in the world in which they do business. With the exception of the United States of America and Canada, the medium in which the business is transacted still remains exclusively sterling.

The Policy

Before the business done at Lloyd's, no matter what its nature, can be brought to completion, it is necessary to issue a policy. The work of preparing the policy is done in the office of the broker who placed the risk, and when prepared the broker sends it up to Lloyd's for signature. All Lloyd's brokers keep a stock of blank policy forms appropriate to the classes of risk insured at Lloyd's.[1] The procedure in the broker's office is for the clerk dealing with a particular case to select the form of policy he requires from stock and to fill in from the slip the details applying to the risk in question. These are, briefly, the name and address of the insured, the amount insured, a description of the property insured, and the term of the policy. Usually all these details will be found on the slip, though if the risk is a complicated one it may be necessary to refer to the original instructions. Any special stipulations expressed on the slip by the under-

[1] A more detailed reference to policy forms appears on pp. 102–114.

writers must be incorporated in the policy, and this is done by attaching the appropriate clauses covering the points in question. The policy must be stamped with the proper stamp duty according to the class of insurance covered, and it is then ready to be signed. The system whereby policies at Lloyd's are signed calls for a special explanation.

Signing. Originally every Lloyd's policy was signed by the individual underwriter accepting the risk. The term "underwriter" is derived from the fact that he *wrote* his name *under* the particulars on the policy to show his acceptance of the risk. In the course of time the signature became that of the underwriting agent of the Syndicate, and this was set against a list of the Names composing the Syndicate with the proportion of the whole line for which each individual Name was responsible. In practice this block of Names was affixed to the policy by a rubber stamp, and the actual signing was often done by a junior clerk, being largely a formality, necessary only to give the policy legal effect, though of course the policy must be signed. When the risk had been placed with more than one Syndicate, each Syndicate agent would sign on the same document. In this the practice differed from that of the companies, for if a risk was placed partly with one company and partly with another each would issue its own policy. At Lloyd's, however, only one policy is issued to which all the underwriters on the risk subscribe. (The marine-insurance companies in London adopted a similar practice in November, 1939, as a wartime measure, and this measure has now become permanent wherever the insured requires a single policy issued by all the companies on the risk.) Under the original system at Lloyd's the broker's clerk would take the policy to the boxes of the various under-

writers and obtain the signature of each in order to complete
his document. This system continued from the inception of
the business, until it was altered during the course of the
First World War.

The Signing Office. In 1916, to economise labour and expense during wartime, the system of each Syndicate's signing its own policies was abandoned, and Lloyd's Underwriters' Signing Bureau, now known as Lloyd's Policy Signing Office, came into existence.[1] An office was set up in Lloyd's
Building to which thereafter all policies had to be taken for
signature, thereby avoiding the necessity to take up the time
of many different underwriters. The signing of each policy
is now done in one operation. A member of the staff of the
Signing Office receives the policy together with the slip showing what underwriting Syndicates are interested and the
share of each. The appropriate rubber-stamped names and
numbers of the Syndicates are then stamped on the policy,
and the signature affixed by the clerk, thus completing the
transaction with the maximum speed and the minimum trouble. The system of attaching a number to each Syndicate
makes it a simple matter for the clerks to pick out the correct
rubber stamp for each Syndicate numbered on the slip.
Scrupulous accuracy in this matter is important as otherwise
policies might be issued bearing the signature of a Syndicate
which had never accepted the risk or omitting a Syndicate
which had.

The saving in both time and labour was found to be so great
that the "Signing Bureau," set up as a wartime expedient,
became a permanent institution and exists today under the
title of Lloyd's Policy Signing Office. Its duties, however,

[1] See Chaps. 6 and 7.

have been extended beyond the original conception and go much further than providing a mere mechanical means of completing signatures. The Lloyd's Policy Signing Office has now an expert staff who carefully check each policy to see that it corresponds with the slip and does not infringe any of the rules which may from time to time be made for the transaction of business at Lloyd's or any State laws. They also keep records of all the policies signed, and lists are furnished daily to underwriters showing the details of the policies signed on their behalf.

The procedure at the Signing Office may be described as follows. When the policy has been prepared in the broker's office and an impressed revenue stamp for the proper stamp duty has been affixed, it is taken by the broker's clerk to Lloyd's Policy Signing Office—at one time housed on the fifth floor in Lloyd's Building but temporarily removed during the war to Pinewood in Buckinghamshire and since at Stafford House in London. The policy must be left, with the slip, in the Signing Office and can be dealt with only in its turn since many thousands of policies go into the office every day. It is perhaps a minor disadvantage of the system that in time of pressure the Signing Office becomes congested, and some delay in obtaining the signed policy may be inevitable. After being left at the Signing Office the policy is first checked with the slip, and should it be incorrect in any particular it is returned to the broker who must clear up the discrepancy with the underwriter before the Signing Office will do anything further with it. If the policy is in order, it is passed to the clerical staff, where the necessary records are made, and the daily lists to underwriters compiled. Originally the policy was then signed by affixing the rub-

ber stamps of the Syndicates and filling in the lines of each.
During the Second World War, however, as a time- and
labour-saving device, a full list of every Syndicate at Lloyd's,
printed in small type, was attached to every Lloyd's policy,
and a Definitive Table printed on the policy indicated the
numbers allocated to those Syndicates which were interested
in the risk and the amount or proportion of their liability. The
Syndicates thus indicated were the only ones operative, in
so far as any particular policy was concerned, the others being entirely inoperative. This system has been continued
after the war, and it is not yet known whether it is to be
considered permanent or whether, in the course of time,
the practice of impressing on the policy by rubber stamp
only the names of the Syndicates interested in a risk will be
resumed. Finally the seal of Lloyd's Policy Signing Office is
embossed on the policy by a machine. Without this seal no
policy which had been signed in the office would be recognised as valid by the underwriters. Although there is nothing
to prevent an underwriter from signing a policy himself, the
practice has now become established that all policies must
bear Lloyd's Policy Signing Office seal.

Policy Forms

It would be outside the scope of this work to deal in detail with all the policy forms issued by Lloyd's Underwriters
but an explanation may be given of their principal features,
so far as these illustrate the nature of the business done at
Lloyd's. In this, the marine and non-marine business must
be dealt with separately. The marine being much the older
may be conveniently examined first.

Marine Form. The whole range of marine insurance in

all its many variations is covered by one basic policy form of very ancient lineage. A copy of this form is reproduced in Fig. 2. To the uninitiated it appears to be almost a meaningless jumble of words, containing much that is unintelligible and some seemingly unnecessary words. This is a superficial view, however, for this form of wording has been built up gradually in the course of past centuries, and every word in it has been devised to meet the demands of actual experience. Its wording is archaic and bears evidence of its seventeenth- and eighteenth-century origin. But the exact meaning of all its clauses has been tested again and again in the English courts, much of it through the judgments of that eminent eighteenth-century judge Lord Mansfield.

This form of policy, after having been evolved over a period of years by the Underwriters at Lloyd's, was revised and confirmed in 1779 in the identical form which is used today. In 1795 an Act of Parliament was passed to amend and consolidate the various laws relating to stamp duties on policies of marine insurance (35 Geo. III c.63). This Act required the Stamp Commissioners to provide printed policies duly stamped for the use of underwriters, and all policies were thereafter required by law to be in the form prescribed by the Act. There were slight differences in the forms to be issued by the two marine corporations, The London Assurance and the Royal Exchange Assurance, and those to be issued by Lloyd's Underwriters, but Lloyd's form was identical with that which had been approved in 1779. Thereafter it became a statutory form and its use was made compulsory by law. This form was re-enacted in the Marine Insurance Act 1906.

The basic form of policy affords a full cover against all

† by the Committee of Lloyd's as entitling the holder to the benefit of the Funds and/or
ty for their distribution unless it bears at foot the Seal of Lloyd's Policy Signing Office.

(No.)

Be it known that

as well in *their* own Name, as for and in the Name and Names of all and every other Person or Persons to whom the same doth, may, or shall appertain, in part or in all, doth make Assurance, and cause *themselves* and them and every of them, to be insured, lost or not lost, at and from

upon any kind of Goods and Merchandises, and also upon the Body, Tackle, Apparel, Ordnance, Munition, Artillery, Boat and other Furniture, of and in the good Ship or Vessel   lied the

whereof is Master, under God, for this present Voyage   or whosoever else shall go for Master in the said Ship, or by whatsoever other Name or Names the same Ship, or the Master thereof, is or shall be named or called, beginning the Adventure upon the said Goods and Merchandises from the loading thereof aboard the said Ship *as above*   upon the said Ship, &c., *as above*

and shall so continue and endure during her Abode there, upon the said Ship, &c.; and further, until the said Ship, with all her Ordnance, Tackle, Apparel, &c., and Goods and Merchandises whatsoever, shall be arrived at *as above*   upon the said Ship, &c., until she hath moored at Anchor Twenty-four Hours in good Safety, and upon the Goods and Merchandises until the same be there discharged and safely landed; and it shall be lawful for the said Ship, &c., in this Voyage to proceed and sail to and touch and stay at any Ports or Places whatsoever *for all purposes*

without Prejudice to this Insurance. The said Ship, &c., Goods and Merchandises, &c., for so much as concerns the Assured by Agreement between the Assured and Assurers   this Policy, are and shall be valued at

TOUCHING the Adventures and Perils which we the Assurers are contented to bear and do take upon us in this Voyage, they are, of the Seas, Men-of-War, Fire, Enemies, Pirates, Rovers, Thieves, Jettisons, Letters of Mart and Countermart, Surprisals, Takings at Sea, Arrests, Restraints and Detainments of all Kings, Princes and People, of what Nation, Condition, or Quality soever, Barratry of the Master and Mariners, and of all other Perils, Losses and Misfortunes that have or shall come to the Hurt, Detriment or Damage of the said Goods and Merchandises and Ship, &c., or any Part thereof; and in case of any Loss or Misfortune, it shall be lawful to the Assured, their Factors, Servants and Assigns, to sue, labour, and travel for, in and about the Defence, Safeguard and Recovery of the said Goods and Merchandises and Ship, &c., or any Part thereof, without Prejudice to this Insurance; to the Charges whereof we, the Assurers, will contribute, each one according to the Rate and Quantity of his Sum herein assured. And it is especially declared and agreed that no acts of the Insurer or Insured in recovering, saving, or preserving the property insured, shall be considered as a waiver or acceptance of abandonment. And it is agreed by us, the Insurers, that this Writing or Policy of Assurance shall be of as much Force and Effect as the surest Writing or Policy of Assurance heretofore made in Lombard Street, or in the Royal Exchange, or elsewhere in London.

LLOYD'S — FOR SIGNATURE BY UNDERWRITING MEMBERS OF LLOYD'S ONLY — UNDERWRITING ACTS 1871 TO 1925

S.G.

Any person not an Underwriting Member of Lloyd's subscribing this Policy, or any person signing for or on behalf of any person so subscribed, will be liable to be proceeded against under Lloyd's Acts.

Printed at Lloyd's, London, England

INSTITUTE DANGEROUS DRUGS CLAUSE.

"It is understood and agreed that no claim under this Policy will be paid in respect of drugs to which the various International Conventions relating to Opium and other dangerous drugs apply unless

(1) the drugs shall be expressly declared to be such in the Policy and the name of the country from which and the name of the country to which they are consigned shall be specifically stated in the Policy

(2) the Proof of Loss is accompanied either by a licence, certificate or authorisation issued by the Government of the country to which the drugs are consigned showing that the importation of the consignment into that country has been approved by a Government or, alternatively, by a licence, certificate or authorisation issued by the Government of the country from which the drugs are consigned showing that the export of the consignment to the destination stated has been approved by that Government; and

(3) the route by which the drugs were conveyed was usual and customary."

Fig. 2. Lloyd's Marine Policy Form.

1. Warranted free of capture, seizure, arrest, restraint or detainment, and the consequences thereof or of any attempt thereat; also from the consequences of hostilities or warlike operations, whether before or after declaration of war or not; but this warranty shall not exclude collision, contact with any fixed or floating object (other than a mine or torpedo), stranding, heavy weather or fire unless caused directly (and independently of the nature of the voyage or service which the vessel concerned or, in the case of a collision, any other vessel involved therein, is performing) by a hostile act by or against a belligerent power; and for the purpose of this warranty "power" includes any authority maintaining naval, military or air forces in association with a power.
Further warranted free from the consequences of civil war, revolution, rebellion, insurrection, or civil strife arising therefrom, or piracy.

2. Warranted free of loss or damage caused by strikers, locked-out workmen or persons taking part in labour disturbances riots or civil commotions.

3. Should the risks excluded by Clause 1 (F.C. & S. Clause) be reinstated in this Policy by deletion of the said Clause, or should the risks or any of them mentioned in the same clause or the risks of mines torpedoes bombs or other engines of war be insured under this Policy, then notwithstanding anything in this Policy to the contrary,

(a) the insurance against the said risks shall not attach to the interest hereby insured or to any part thereof

(i) prior to being on board an oversea vessel,

(ii) [For the purpose of this Clause an oversea vessel shall be deemed to mean a vessel carrying the interest from one port or place to another where such voyage involves a sea passage by that vessel]

(iii) after being discharged overside from an oversea vessel at the final port of discharge.

after expiry of 15 days counting from midnight of the day on which the oversea vessel is safely anchored or moored at the final port of discharge, whichever shall first occur,

(iii) at a port or place of transhipment to another oversea vessel after expiry of 15 days counting from midnight of the day on which the oversea vessel entering with the interest is safely anchored or moored until the interest is on board the on-carrying oversea vessel.

In the event of the exercise of any liberty granted to the Shipowner or Charterer under the contract of affreightment whereby such contract is terminated at a port or place other than the destination named therein, such port or place shall be deemed the final port of discharge for the purpose of this Clause 3.

(b) this Policy is warranted free of any claim based upon loss of, or frustration of, the insured voyage or adventure caused by arrests restraints or detainments of Kings Princes Peoples Usurpers or persons attempting to usurp power.

If anything contained in this Policy shall be inconsistent with Clause 3 (a) and 3 (b) or either of them it shall to the extent of such inconsistency be null and void.

And so we, the Assurers, are contented, and do hereby promise and bind ourselves, each one for his own Part, our Heirs, Executors, and Goods, to the Assured, their Executors, Administrators, and Assigns, for the true Performance of the Premises, confessing ourselves paid the Consideration due unto us for this Assurance by the Assured at and after the Rate of

IN WITNESS whereof we, the Assurers, have subscribed our Names and Sums assured in LONDON,

as hereinafter appears.

N.B.—Corn, Fish, Salt, Fruit, Flour, and Seed are warranted free from Average, unless general, or the Ship be stranded; Sugar, Tobacco, Hemp, Flax, Hides, and Skins are warranted free from Average, under Five Pounds per Cent.; and all other Goods, also the Ship and Freight, are warranted free from Average, under Three Pounds per Cent., unless general, or the Ship be stranded.

NOW KNOW YE, that We the Assurers, members of the Syndicate(s) whose definitive Number(s) in the attached list are set out in the Table overleaf, or attached overleaf, hereby bind Ourselves, each for his own part and not one for another, and in respect of his due proportion only, to pay or make good to the Assured all such Loss and/or Damage which he or they may sustain by any one or more of the aforesaid perils, and so that the due proportion for which each of Us the Assurers is liable shall be ascertained by reference to his proportion of the total Sum assured which is in the said Table set opposite the definitive Number of the Syndicate of which such Assurer is a member.

IN WITNESS whereof the Manager of Lloyd's Policy Signing Office has subscribed his Name on behalf of each of Us.

LLOYD'S POLICY SIGNING OFFICE.

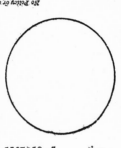

In the event of accident whereby loss or damage may result in a claim under this Policy, the settlement will be much facilitated if immediate notice be given to the nearest Lloyd's Agent.

MANAGER.

(13-11-899) (15-6-43) 23-1-47 MZl

Fig. 2. (Continued)

Definitive Numbers of Syndicates and Amount, Percentage or Proportion of the Total Amount assured shared between the Members of those Syndicates.

Amount, Percentage or Proportion.	Syndicate No.	Underwriters' Reference.	Amount, Percentage or Proportion.	Syndicate No.	Underwriters' Reference.	Amount, Percentage or Proportion.	Syndicate No.	Underwriters' Reference.

Fig. 2. (Continued)

& Co., Ltd.

LLOYD'S LONDON

INCORPORATED BY ACT OF PARLIAMENT

In the event of accident whereby loss or damage may result in a claim under this Policy, the settlement will be much facilitated if immediate notice be given to the nearest Lloyd's Agent.)

Fig. 2. (*Continued*)

the perils of the sea, but if it contains the *F. C. & S.* (Free from Capture and Seizure) *Clause* the effect is to exclude war risks. Where the F. C. & S. Clause in the policy is deleted so as to restore the cover against war risks, the *Frustration Clause,* reading "Warranted free of any claim based upon loss of, or frustration of, the insured voyage or adventure caused by arrests, restraints or detainments of Kings Princes Peoples Usurpers or persons attempting to usurp power," comes into operation.

This clause was added after the First World War to meet the circumstances set up by the case of *Sanday v. British & Foreign Marine Insurance Co. Ltd.* This case concerned shipments destined for Germany at the time war broke out. To continue the voyage would have been illegal so the shipments were diverted to a British port. The assured claimed a total loss, although the cargo was intact, undamaged, and available to him, on the ground that the voyage (which was insured under the marine policy) had been lost. Underwriters resisted the claim, but litigation taken up to the House of Lords resulted in a judgment against them. It was never the intention that such loss should be covered by the marine policy so the Frustration Clause was drafted and is now in every Lloyd's marine policy. It is, however, an added clause and is not part of the actual policy wording which, as stated above, remains identical with that adopted by Lloyd's in 1779, and which is the policy wording to be found in the Schedule of the Marine Insurance Act 1906.

Lloyd's marine policies contain the letters "S.G." placed above the amount insured. The exact significance of these letters was for some time the subject of much controversy, but it can now be said with certainty that they stand for

Ship and Goods. It would seem that there were originally three forms of practically identical policy, one covering ship only, one goods only, and one both ship and goods, the only differences being the omission of certain words not applicable to the kind of insurance. The form applicable to ship only bore the letter "S" and that covering goods only the letter "G," but when the form was finally settled in 1779 it bore both the letters "S.G." and has so remained ever since.

For many years, up to about the end of the eighteenth century, the standard form of policy was used for all insurances on ships or cargoes. With the development of business throughout the world, the one form of policy became in course of time insufficient by itself to provide for the many different conditions, such as voyage routes, nature of cargo, and extra hazards incurred. It became necessary to amplify or limit the cover granted under the plain policy form, and this is done by the addition of clauses or warranties or both. This does not mean that any new policy forms were devised. The original policy form remains unaltered, but its operation is varied by the attachment of gummed slips giving the clauses in general use or the clauses or warranties required in any particular case.

As already mentioned, the standard clauses in their present form were drafted by the Institute of London Underwriters and are the result of the combined experience of the marine market. Their exact purport and effect may be learnt from the textbooks on the subject.

By attaching clauses, the original Lloyd's marine-policy form is adapted to special circumstances. Thus there are clauses which extend the scope of the cover such as the *Running Down Clause* covering a shipowner in respect of a part of his liability due to collisions. The standard form of policy which is designed to apply to a single voyage may be required to cover a time insurance, and the necessary variations are provided by the *Institute Time Clauses,* applicable to the insurance of hulls. For cargo insurances the *Institute Cargo Clauses* and special clauses suited to the insured interest will be attached.

In addition to clauses, the cover may also be varied by attaching the *Institute Warranties.* These warranties impose certain restrictions on the scope of the cover granted under the policy and with two exceptions are of a geographical nature. They may exclude liability altogether while the ship is in certain defined areas of the globe, or they may permit voyages in various areas only at certain periods of the year. The exceptions relate to Indian coal which may not be carried during the hot season and Polish coal which may not be carried on European voyages south of Cape Finisterre. The purpose of these warranties is to exclude from the normal policy at the normal rate of premium certain risks of a hazardous nature which could only be accepted at special rates commensurate with the higher risks involved.

The examples given are meant to illustrate the manner in which marine policies are drafted in the business done at Lloyd's, and no attempt is made to give a complete or detailed account of the many provisions and variations in the form of policy required to give effect to the many kinds of marine cover which exist in modern practice. These are all to be found in the textbooks on the subject.

One other provision in the policy is the "N.B." printed at the end of the policy form (see page 105). This is commonly known as the *Memorandum,* and though it now appears as part of the original policy and was so included in the revised form of 1779, in fact it is a clause added to a form of policy originally existing without it. The memorandum is known to have come into established use at Lloyd's in 1749, though it was used in various forms before that. Its purpose is to restrict the underwriters' liability in regard to certain kinds of merchandise, which are particularly susceptible to damage by sea water. Its provisions are today extended and amplified by the clauses in common use.

By the Marine Insurance Act 1906, it is provided that every marine insurance must be expressed in a policy, and no time policy may be issued for a longer period than 12 months. One effect of this is that there is no system of renewing marine policies by means of renewal receipts as is the common practice in non-marine business. Whenever a marine insurance has to be renewed, a new policy is issued even if the new policy covers identically the same risk as the old. Voyage policies and cargo insurances run usually for a specified period less than a year and do not usually require renewal on the same lines. For time policies covering hulls renewals will be effected from year to year on substantially the same policy conditions, but in every case a new policy is issued each year.

Every policy of marine insurance must be stamped with an impressed inland revenue stamp. The law on this point is laid down in the Stamp Act 1891 under which a scale of stamp duties is provided, the amount varying according to the nature of the policy, whether time or voyage or cargo, and according to the sum insured under the policy. No marine-insurance policy is valid unless properly stamped, whether the policy be for direct insurance or for reinsurance.

Non-marine Forms. Policies issued for non-marine business at Lloyd's differ widely from those issued for marine business. They are of course quite modern, drafted from time to time as required. There is no ancient original document, gradually taking shape over the centuries, nor is there any kind of statutory form of which the use is obligatory. The risks insured are of many different kinds ranging over all branches of insurance business other than marine and life. In theory there is nothing to prevent each underwriter from drawing up his own form of policy for each of the different kinds of risk he insures, but in practice most non-marine policy forms have been standardised and are used by all underwriters engaged in the business. These standard forms have been drawn up under the authority of Lloyd's Underwriters' Fire and Non-Marine Association, and there are separate forms for each of the classes of non-marine business which show the headings and preamble common to all the forms, and also the operative clause binding the underwriters to insure and the form of attestation completing the contract. The body of the policy contains the special wording appropriate to the kind of risk insured. This wording is in a simple form and the conditions are reduced to a minimum. Forms for other classes of non-marine business have been developed from the fire form and in some cases are more complicated with many additional clauses and conditions necessary to give effect to the intention of the contract. It is the general rule, with only a few exceptions, to include all clauses and conditions in the body of the contract before the attestation clause, and not to follow the practice common in the company world of printing the clauses on the face of the policy and the conditions on the back.

Standard non-marine policy forms fall into the following groups:

(a) Fire
(b) Burglary
(c) All risks
(d) Personal Accident
(e) Liability and Indemnity
(f) Miscellaneous

Each form of policy is given a distinguishing letter, which is a convenience for reference on slips and cover notes. As far as possible the various forms within each group bear the same letter, with a number added to distinguish them. Thus all personal accident policies bear the letter "K" and are numbered "K1," "K2," "K3," etc., to show the different forms. These numbers on a slip or cover note denote the exact scope of the insurance required. Among fire policies there is some variation; commercial forms are lettered "C," private-house forms "F," profits insurance "M," adjustable policies "N," and replacement policies "S." A general form of policy for miscellaneous risks bears the letter "J." There is no particular system in the allocation of letters, which have been attached to policy forms as required, but to those accustomed to working in the non-marine market the meaning of each letter is immediately recognised.

For many classes of insurance only one form of policy is necessary, such as all-risks insurance, cash in transit, or pub-

lic liability, but in personal-accident insurance there are 6
forms, in burglary insurance 10 forms, and in the fire group 15.
These are necessary to provide for the varying scope of the
cover. Thus the fire group of policies includes four commercial forms, one private-house form, five profits-insurance
forms, four adjustable-insurance forms, and one replacement-
insurance form.

It would be outside the scope of this work to deal in detail with all the different forms of policy issued through the
non-marine market at Lloyd's. Their terms and conditions
are of a technical nature, dependent upon the class of insurance to which they relate. They follow the established principles and practice of cash class of business and are more
fully described in the sectional insurance textbooks.

The Proposal

The development of non-marine insurance with its many
widely differing types has led to the increasing use of proposal forms. In marine insurance proposal forms are not used.
Since the business is more uniform in character, conducted
only with business houses, on facts which are more or less of
public knowledge, the proposal form is not necessary. Non-
marine business is of great diversity, conducted with both
business people and private individuals. It depends upon
many unknown factors which must be disclosed to the underwriters and which can best be elicited by the answers to the
questions contained in a proposal form.

Proposal forms have therefore been drawn up in standard
wordings to apply to the principal forms of non-marine insurance. These are not used, however, in every case without
exception. They would not usually be asked for in a simple

fire or burglary proposal on a private house or shop risk. In such cases the broker would submit the particulars for insurance on a slip. But in such instances as personal-accident, motor-car, employers'-liability, all-risks, livestock, public-liability, or the more complicated commercial fire and burglary risks, a proposal form is invariably required. The intending insured must fill up this form, giving all the required information, and it is then attached to the slip for the underwriters' consideration. His initial on the slip will be given as incorporating the proposal form to be the basis of the contract to be insured.

Although the proposal forms are drafted on as simple a basis as possible, the questions are necessarily comprehensive so as to bring out all the information required by the underwriters to enable them to form a judgment on the merits of the risk and its eligibility for acceptance.

Clauses

It frequently happens in non-marine business that special conditions have to be attached to the policy to provide for the particular circumstances of a given risk. Such special conditions are embodied in *clauses* of which a large number have been drafted under the authority of Lloyd's Underwriters' Fire and Non-Marine Association. Such clauses will be attached as required to the normal form of policy applicable to the risk insured and either may be restrictive in character by excluding certain risks or limiting the scope of the cover or may extend the cover by including certain perils not ordinarily insured or agreeing to certain conditions not found in the normal policy form. An example of the way in which these clauses operate is given in the *Service of Suit*

Clause applicable to insurances in the United States of America which reads as follows:

It is agreed that in the event of the failure of Underwriters hereon to pay any amount claimed to be due hereunder, Underwriters hereon, at the request of the Assured, will submit to the jurisdiction of any Court of competent jurisdiction within the United States and will comply with all requirements necessary to give such Court jurisdiction and all matters arising hereunder shall be determined in accordance with the law and practice of such Court.

It is further agreed that service of process in such suit may be made upon

, and
that in any suit instituted against any one of them upon this contract, Underwriters will abide by the final decision of such Court or of any Appellate Court in the event of an appeal.

The above-named are authorised and directed to accept service of process on behalf of Underwriters in any such suit and/or upon the Assured's request to give a written undertaking to the Assured that they will enter a general appearance upon Underwriters' behalf in the event such a suit shall be instituted.

At the present time there are some 135 of these special clauses in use, and their number is from time to time added to as the development of the business demands.

Stamps

All policies issued at Lloyd's must be stamped, so as to comply with the revenue laws. The stamping of insurance policies is governed in general by the Stamp Act 1906.

For marine-insurance policies a scale of stamp duties is laid down in the Act, varying according to the kind of policy, whether time or voyage or cargo, and based to some extent *ad valorem* on the sum insured. For policies insuring against loss or damage to property (other than marine) the stamp duty was fixed at 1d., which has since been increased to 6d. (Finance Act 1920). This applies to fire or burglary policies and is a flat rate irrespective of the sum insured. An insurance against third-party liability must be stamped with a 6d. stamp, as an agreement to indemnify. Where the insurance combines damage to property with liability as in the householder's comprehensive policy, both duties are payable, and the stamp must be 1/–d.

Policy Period

The period for which policies are issued at Lloyd's varies according to the class of insurance. In the marine department the policy is issued for the period of the voyage and expires as soon as the voyage is completed. There is an exception to this in the insurance of hulls which are generally covered under policies for periods of time, usually for 12 calendar months. In the non-marine department all policies will run for 1 year, or for a shorter period if required, but will not run for more than 1 year. This rule has been relaxed in recent years to allow additional odd time to take this insurance to a quarter day when the insured desires it. The quarter-day system has always been a strong feature of British fire insurance. This system provides that all policies shall be made renewable at one of the four quarter days, viz., Ladyday (March 25th), Midsummer (June 24th), Michaelmas (September 29th), and Christmas (December 25th). This was never absolutely exclusive, however. Under modern practice it has become quite frequent for Lloyd's Underwriters to issue policies on a long-term basis, up to perhaps as much as 5 years, but this is only done where required to meet special needs. There is good reason for restricting the issue of policies to a period of 1 year, because this facilitates the keeping of each year's accounts separately and avoids any difficulty in winding up long-term obligations when there are changes in a Syndicate.

Renewal

As already mentioned, the practice in marine insurance is to issue new policies on the expiry of an existing policy and not to renew by way of renewal receipt. On the extension of Lloyd's activities into the non-marine market the same practice was followed, and though insurances might be continued year after year on exactly the same terms, a new policy would be issued each year. At one time this practice was universal, but in recent years it has become more common, to save both labour and paper, to issue renewal receipts in lieu of new policies, where there is no material alteration in the scope of the insurance. The renewal receipt should be attached by the insured to the original policy. Two forms of renewal receipts are in general use, specimens of which are shown in Figs. 3 and 4. *Renewal receipt A* is the simpler form and is used only when there has been no change in the names of the underwriters comprising the Syndicates responsible for the renewal. This receipt gives brief details of the policy and acknowledges the receipt of the renewal premium. *Renewal receipt B* is for use when there has been a change in the names in the Syndicate. This receipt sets out a short operative clause whereby the new names accept their share of the insurance in terms of the original policy, and the new syndicate is

A

This Receipt should be attached to the Original Policy.

No Policy or other Contract dated on or after 1st Jan., 1924, will be recognised by the Committee of Lloyd's as entitling the holder to the benefit of the Funds and/or Guarantees lodged by the Underwriters of the Policy or Contract as security for their liabilities unless it bears at foot the Seal of Lloyd's Policy Signing Office.

Form approved by
Lloyd's Underwriters' Fire and
Non-Marine Association.

LLOYD'S, LONDON.

RENEWAL RECEIPT No.................

(Signed by Underwriting Members of Lloyd's only.)

Policy No.	Name of Assured.	Renewal Date.	Sum Insured.	Premium.

RECEIVED the.................. day of.................. 19......, the Premium as stated hereon for the

renewal of the above.................. Policy for ONE YEAR from the renewal date.

(SEAL)

Fig. 3. Renewal receipt A.

B

This Document should be attached to the Original Policy.

No Policy or other Contract dated on or after 1st Jan., 1924, will be recognised by the Committee of Lloyd's as entitling the Holder to the benefit of the Funds and/or Guarantees lodged by the Underwriters of the Policy or Contract as security for their liabilities unless it bears at foot of Lloyd's Policy Signing Office.

LLOYD'S

RENEWAL POLICY AND RECEIPT No................

(Signed by Underwriting Members of Lloyd's only.)

SUM INSURED HEREON ....

Form approved by Lloyd's Underwriters' Fire and Non-Marine Association.

Any person not an Underwriting Member of Lloyd's subscribing this Policy, or any person uttering the same if so subscribed, will be liable to be proceeded against under Lloyd's Acts.

Printed at Lloyd's, London, England.

Assured ....

In consideration of the payment of .... (the receipt of which is hereby acknowledged), We, the Underwriters, members of the Syndicate(s) of which is/are set out in the Table overleaf, or attached overleaf, hereby agree, each for his own part and not one for Another, and in respect of his due proportion only, to hold the Assured covered during the period of TWELVE MONTHS from .... to .... Policy

.... (including any endorsements thereon) dated the .... day of .... 19 ...... and numbered ....

and so that the due proportion for which each of us the Underwriters is liable shall be the share set against his name as a member of the relevant Syndicate in the list hereinafter referred to of the Amount, Percentage or Proportion of the total sum assured which is in the said Table set opposite the definitive number of the Syndicate of which such Underwriter is a member.

In Witness whereof the Manager of Lloyd's Policy Signing Office has subscribed his Name on behalf of each of Us.

LLOYD'S POLICY SIGNING OFFICE,

DATED IN LONDON this................

MANAGER.

Fig. 4. Renewal receipt B.

NAMES AND SHARES OF THE UNDERWRITERS.

The name of the Underwriters being members of the Syndicate(s) the definitive number(s) of which is/are set out in the Table above referred to are set out in a list entitled "List of Underwriting Members of Lloyd's showing their respective Syndicates and shares therein," as at the date hereof, which is filed with the Lloyd's Policy Signing Office and is available for inspection by the Assured and which shall be deemed to be incorporated in and to form part of this policy. A certified true copy of the list or at the assured's option of the material parts of the list under the signature of the Manager of the Lloyd's Policy Signing Office will be furnished to the Assured on application and shall be binding and conclusive upon the Underwriters.

The Table above referred to being a Table showing

(a) the definitive numbers of the Syndicates the members of which are parties to this Insurance; and

(b) the amounts underwritten for, or the percentage or proportion of the total sum insured underwritten for each Syndicate and shared among its members.

6.5.48

(SEAL)

Definitive Numbers of Syndicates and Amount, Percentage or Proportion of the Total Amount assured shared between the Members of those Syndicates.

Amount, Percentage or Proportion.	Syndicate No.	Underwriters' Reference.	Amount, Percentage or Proportion.	Syndicate No.	Underwriters' Reference.	Amount, Percentage or Proportion.	Syndicate No.	Underwriters' Reference.

Fig. 4. (Continued)

noted on the receipt. The seal of Lloyd's Policy Signing Office must be affixed to both receipts.

Accounts

The accounting systems used by Lloyd's Underwriters in the practice of their business are their own domestic concern and may be carried on in any way which permits them to comply with the requirements of the annual audit. It is the universal rule, however, for accounts to be kept on a 3-year basis. Each year's underwriting account is kept quite distinct from any other year and remains open for 3 years, *i.e.*, for the year of account and the two following years. During that period all premiums belonging to that year's underwriting are credited to that account. These may arise from policies closed after the end of the year or from additional premiums charged on any of the year's policies. Similarly all return premiums allowed on that year's policies are debited to the account, as are all claims paid. It is an essential feature of the system that all claim payments are referred back to the year's account to which the policy belongs, provided that the payment is made within the 3-year period. At the end of that period a balance is struck and a reserve is set up to provide for any claims still remaining to be settled and for any possible claims still to be notified. The ultimate surplus is then available for distribution as profit to the members of the Syndicate. This system avoids the necessity to set up reserves for unexpired risks, since every risk will have expired before the end of the 3-year period, while it greatly simplifies the task of constructing a reliable reserve for outstanding claims, as the majority of these will have been settled during the period.

Chapter 5. CLAIMS PROCEDURE

While the detail of claims settlement at Lloyd's has under-gone considerable change during the past 25 years, the funda-mental procedure has not changed.

This fundamental procedure is, on broad lines, that as soon as an assured becomes aware that his insured interest has incurred loss or damage, or even that it has been involved in a casualty in which it may have been lost or damaged, he notifies his broker, who, in turn, notifies the underwriters. In the event that a claim is *prima facie* of a minor nature, the initial advice may be given only to the leading underwriters, but if the claim is likely to be for a total loss or a serious par-tial loss, each individual underwriter is advised. This applies equally to marine and non-marine business which share, to some extent, the broad lines of claims-settlement practice though each has its own detail.

Marine Claims

Taking marine business first, when a claim is brought to the notice of the leading underwriter, he considers what course he should pursue. It should be understood that gen-erally an underwriter (*i.e.,* an underwriting agent) does not deal with claims personally, but has a claims adjuster, a clerk of experience in claims procedure to whom notification is made and who, subject to the ultimate decision in certain cases by the underwriter, has plenipotentiary authority to deal with claims. In recent times the institution of Lloyd's Underwriters' Claims Office (see pages 165–169) had modified this practice, but while the Claims Office settles claims on behalf of those underwriters who entrust this duty to it, many of these also have a claims adjuster who deals with doubtful and borderline cases which are referred to them by the Claims Office for consideration.

It is to the claims adjuster that notice of a claim is given, subsequent procedure depending largely on the nature of the claim. In the case of hull and cargo risks it is very common for the leading underwriter to endorse the written notification "Instruct Salvage Association" and to append his initial, the underwriters who subsequently see the notification adding their initials in turn, so that there is a common endorsement to the effect that the Salvage Association shall take charge of the matter and deal with it in the interest of all concerned, assured, insurer, and any other party to the insurance or involved in the casualty.

The Salvage Association [1] then deals with the matter as required. If it is a claim on a ship that has stranded, the Association will instruct a surveyor to proceed to the stranding place, and at the same time negotiations will be commenced with a view to refloating the vessel. These will involve the hiring of salvage tugs and plant, and perhaps the employment of barges or lighters into which cargo or bunkers can be discharged. Whatever is necessary to be done the Salvage Association will do and will keep underwriters advised by means of notifications which are circulated to those interested from time to time. In the case of a claim on cargo, the procedure is similar. A surveyor is instructed

[1] See pp. 169–174.

to make a survey and report, and such steps as are necessary to salve the cargo or to dispose of it if it is unsalvable
are taken by those who are expert in such matters. The
principle is that the Salvage Association acts on behalf of
underwriters to protect their interests and also take steps to
minimise loss or damage to the subject matter insured. The
representative of the Association may, and frequently does,
collaborate with the representative of the assured, holding
joint surveys and generally consulting him as to the means
of salvage to be employed. This applies equally to all kinds
of casualty, stranding, fire, collision, heavy-weather damage,
or any loss or damage resulting from a peril insured against.
In the case of minor claims, this process may be unnecessary.
A simple statement by the assured, accompanied by such
documentary evidence as may be required, will generally be
accepted by the underwriters as proof of the nature and
extent of the claim, and in such cases the broker can render
very considerable assistance in preparing the documents and
working out the necessary calculations.

Thus far only the preliminaries to the settlement of a
claim have been considered. The actual process of settlement varies in different circumstances. In the case of a
straightforward *particular average* on cargo it may not be
necessary to employ an *average adjuster*, and the work of
preparing the claim can be, and generally is, carried out in
the office of the broker who is entrusted with its collection.
He is not necessarily the broker who placed the insurance,
although he generally is because the common practice is for
the assured to deal with one firm of brokers. If, as in certain
cases, an assured employs more than one firm of brokers, he
would ask only the firm that placed a risk to collect a claim

on that risk. Only if an assured has changed brokers would he require his new broker to collect a claim on a policy effected by the broker who previously handled his business.

If a claim is complex, even if a *general average* is not involved, an average adjuster will be employed, and here, perhaps, it would be well to deal briefly with particular average, general average, and the status and functions of an average adjuster.

Particular and General Average. It is customary in marine insurance to describe particular average by saying it is not general average. The Marine Insurance Act lays down that "A Particular Average loss is a partial loss of the subject matter insured, caused by a peril insured against, and which is not a General Average loss." The traditional marine policy in the "Memorandum" warrants the subject matter insured "free from Average unless General." This negative definition, while comprehensive and unlikely to lead to technical difficulties, is not very enlightening.

Broadly speaking *average* is loss or damage. The word has no association with that spelt in the same way meaning a mean or proportion. Gow attributes it to the medieval Latin *averagium* meaning a loss in transit, such as leakage, but he also mentions a possible attribution to an Arabic word *awar* meaning defect.

In an elementary sense particular average is just straightforward damage resulting from the action of the wind or sea, as, for instance, the carrying away of a sail or rigging, damage by sea water entering a hold as a result of heavy seas sweeping the deck, or damage caused by a stranding or collision. Fire damage too can be particular average, and, accepting this broad general definition, the aptness of the negative definition of the Marine Insurance Act becomes apparent.

General average is defined in the Marine Insurance Act in the following words: "A general average loss is a loss caused by or directly consequential upon a general average act. It includes a general average expenditure as well as a general average sacrifice. . . ." This necessitates a definition of a *general-average act* which is, "There is a general average act where any extraordinary sacrifice or expenditure is voluntarily and reasonably made or incurred in time of peril for the purpose of preserving the property imperilled in the common adventure."

A straightforward example of a general-average sacrifice would be the cutting away of a mast to ease a ship imperilled by heavy weather. This would be a sacrifice voluntarily and reasonably made. Another example would be damage to a ship's engines caused by working them in an endeavour to refloat her from a stranding. This would be *incurred*, rather than *made*, and is an example of the reason for the alternatives of the wording of the definition quoted above.

The important feature of a general-average act is that it must be done for the preservation of the interests in the common adventure. These interests are ship, cargo, and, in most cases, freight.

General average also includes expenditure consequent upon a general-average act.

General average, as such, has nothing to do with marine insurance, but the marine-insurance policy usually indemnifies the assured against his liability for general average.

The essential feature of general average is that it imposes on the interests in a common adventure the sharing of sacrifices made for the preservation of the adventure as a whole. In the case of a mast cut away to save ship and cargo from sinking, the cargo would be required to contribute to the necessary repairs in proportion to its value, the ship bearing its own proportion according to its value.

It will be seen that there is sound common sense in the negative definition of particular average as being a partial loss caused by a peril insured against that is not general average.

If a general average affected only two elementary values, say a ship valued at £5,000 and a cargo valued at £3,000, adjustment would be a very simple matter. If, say, a mast and rigging cost £80 to replace after a general-average sacrifice, the cost would be shared in proportion to the values involved, and the ship would pay £50 and the cargo £30.

In practice such a simple case would never arise. In modern sea transport so many interests may be involved and so many intricacies of valuation and niceties of law may have to be considered that a special profession of average adjuster has come into being. In Great Britain these are members of an Association and are qualified by examination, and while the Association has no Charter, and the profession is not a close one in the sense that medicine and the law are, nevertheless practice in average adjusting is practically confined to its members.

If it is necessary to have a claim adjusted by an average adjuster, all the necessary documents are submitted to him. These documents are the ship's log, containing the record of the casualty and all papers concerning the cargo, freight, etc. Then all accounts of expenditure, survey reports, etc., are required, and in short every document or record having any bearing on the matter, including of course any policies of insurance involved. The adjuster draws up a statement showing the total amount of loss and expenditure separated into general average and particular average and, where necessary, any items to be debited to the shipowner as being for his own account, as, for instance, any work carried out for him not included in the claim, not covered by insurance, or not payable by underwriters from any cause.

This statement is the basic document on which claims of this nature are settled. It has been said that in comparatively simple claims the services of an adjuster are not necessary, the settlement being adjusted in the broker's office. Whether there is adjustment by an average adjuster or not, the procedure of actual settlement and collection of a claim is identical. First the policy is endorsed with the brief particulars of the claim: "settled herein a claim for General and Particular Average £2,875. £1. 9. 7%" would be a typical endorsement. The policy thus endorsed is then submitted to the leading underwriter, or, if the leading underwriter is a member of Lloyd's Underwriters' Claims Office, to that office. The *Statement of Adjustment* and other documents substantiating the claim accompany the policy, and after scrutiny the claim is either settled, or if there be some question as to any detail of it, the broker is consulted and the point at issue discussed with him. Eventually, save where irreconcilable differences arise, the claim will be settled, either as originally endorsed or as amended by agreement. If irreconcilable differences arise, it may be necessary to have recourse to arbitration or litigation. Indeed the bulk of marine-insurance law has been created out of precedents made by legal decisions on disputed points. That these precedents have been embodied in the Marine Insurance Act 1906 in no way negatives this statement, for the Act is largely if not entirely a codification of case law previous to its enactment and is, indeed, so good a codification that it has never been the subject of any litigation arising out of its provisions.

Assuming, however, that no question arises, a claim is settled by the underwriter's initialling the policy in the same way that a slip is initialled when a risk is underwritten. This is the pledge that the underwriter will pay the claim. The details of the claim are entered in the underwriters' books and in due course the amount settled by the underwriter is paid.

Claim Payments. In the early nineteenth century, the custom of Lloyd's was to settle accounts annually, balancing claims against premiums, the party, broker, or underwriter in whose favour there was a credit balance being paid by the other party. Since even in those days total losses were paid separately, it was almost invariably the case that the balance was in favour of the underwriter. To encourage early settlement, underwriters used to allow brokers a discount of 10 per cent of the amount due if the account was settled on or before January 8th. This, it would seem, is the origin of the 10 per cent discount on premiums now by custom allowed to the assured in English practice. At Lloyd's it is now the custom to settle accounts quarterly, a statement being prepared by the broker showing the amount of premiums due to and the amount of claims due from an underwriter for the past 3 months. Total losses, however, are generally paid within 8 days of settlement by individual payment. This means that the usual quarterly account generally has a balance in favour of the underwriter, and the broker either pays that balance or the underwriter and broker exchange cheques, each paying the full amount debited to him in the statement. In the marine-insurance-company market, while the general procedure of claims settlement is identical with that at Lloyd's, payment is on a different basis, the companies rendering monthly accounts for premiums and paying claims weekly. No accounts are rendered by brokers to companies for claims, in the ordinary way, each company paying, weekly, the claims settled during the preceding week. Only when differences in accounting arise is there any necessity for the making up of an account, and such differences are usually resolved by a checking of details between the accountancy departments of the broker and the company concerned.

So far as the assured is concerned, this domestic arrangement by which Lloyd's Underwriters pay claims quarterly and the companies weekly does not have any effect. Brokers pay their clients as and when a claim is due to be paid, irrespective of whether the money has or has not been received from the underwriter. That is why it is customary to pay total losses within 8 days of settlement. A broker can usually finance the payment of claims to his clients without difficulty, but because to find perhaps hundreds of thousands of pounds to pay for one serious total loss might require recourse to a bank, brokers are customarily placed in funds in respect of total losses in order that they may have the resources necessary to enable them to pay their clients on the due date.

The settlement of claims both at Lloyd's and by the marine-insurance companies requires a very deep technical knowledge of marine-insurance law and practice, and the best technicians of the business are to be found in the claims departments as a rule.

Having been settled a claim becomes the raw material of a good deal of an underwriter's statistics. Most, if not all underwriters compile statistics, those of the marine companies being, as a rule, more elaborate and more detailed than those of Lloyd's Underwriters.

Statistics. In compiling such statistics it is the general custom to analyse claims so that it can be seen at a glance what proportion of a claim is particular average, what general average, and what is debitable to the cover of the marine policy against liabilities, such as the liability for damage done to another vessel in collision. Many and various systems of statistics are in use in the market, but almost invariably *fleet* figures are kept showing the premiums and claims attaching to the accounts of individual shipowners and shipping lines. Bulk statistics showing the premiums received and the claims paid are also kept, so that an underwriter can see, at any given time, the state of his underwriting account, but the variations of statistical systems are many, and it would require a volume to deal with them in any detail.

One more point. An underwriter's initial appended to an endorsement of a claim on a policy is as sacred as his initial on a slip. It pledges him to pay the claim on the due date, and there is no case on record of an underwriter having failed to honour his initial once it has been appended by proper authority to an endorsement.

Non-marine Claims

Claims under non-marine business are not dealt with under any uniform system. Policies issued through the non-marine branch are of many different types, and the claims arising thereunder differ in like manner. Different considerations will arise in the conduct of, say, fire claims, or burglary claims, or personal-accident claims, or as the case may be, and no settled procedure can be laid down. The insured must notify his claim to the broker who in turn advises the underwriters. Usually the leading underwriter decides how the claim is to be dealt with, the remaining underwriters on the risk being willing to follow the lead. The insured must, of course, submit reasonable evidence of his loss and proof that it was due to a peril insured against under the policy. If this is done to the satisfaction of the leading underwriter, settlement may be authorised without further formality, but this would be done only for small claims. When any substantial amount is involved, or where there is any doubt as to the nature or extent of the liability, the underwriters will appoint an *assessor* to deal with the claim, and settlement will be made on his report. When the amount of the claim has been agreed, the settlement is endorsed on the policy and initialled by the underwriters. Payment is then made by a credit to the broker's account, who in turn pays the amount due to the insured.

Chapter 6. LLOYD'S SERVICES

The Corporation of Lloyd's provides many and useful services for its members, acting, as a Corporation, in the role of guide, philosopher, and friend and, further, carrying out on behalf of the members duties and operations which are not, in themselves, integral with a contract of insurance but which have a very close association with the business. Some of the services are of a general nature and some are particular while others are a combination of the general and the particular. These services, a description of which is given in the succeeding pages, will be dealt with under the following headings:

Lloyd's Agents
The *Shipping Index* and Other Publications
Lloyd's Form of Salvage Agreement
Lloyd's Policy Signing Office
Lloyd's Underwriters' Claims Office
Claims Payable Abroad and the Average Department
The Salvage Association
Lloyd's Register

Lloyd's Agents

Perhaps the most important service available to the members is the system of Lloyd's *Agents* which spreads like a network all over the maritime world, excepting communist countries, and which paradoxically does not operate as representing Lloyd's Underwriters as a whole although an individual agent may act as the representative of underwriters in cases where he has received specific instructions with regard to a particular insurance.

Origin

Fully to appreciate the place of Lloyd's agency system in the organisation of Lloyd's it is necessary to go back to the Coffee House days, when Edward Lloyd provided his customers with the reports of ships' movements which he had gathered from his correspondents and others as part of his business as a coffee-house proprietor. By 1788 a system had developed under which Lloyd's Coffee House received reports from a number of correspondents in the principal ports of the British Isles who, by a special arrangement with the Post Office, sent in their reports of arrivals, departures, and casualties in envelopes addressed to the Postmaster General with the word "Lloyd's" in the corner. This arrangement was made possible by the system then existing under which the Post Office officials looked to perquisites rather than to their salaries for the greater part of their incomes. The letters being addressed to the Postmaster General, no postage was paid on them, but the Master of Lloyd's Coffee House paid annually the sum of £200, which was usually shared by the Secretary of the Post Office and the Comptroller General of the Inland Revenue Department.

This arrangement saved the Coffee House a postage bill that would have been prohibitive in cost at the rates then current, and since the letters addressed to the Postmaster General were opened immediately upon their arrival and

handed to a messenger from the Coffee House, the news
contained in them became available to the members hours
before it would have arrived in the ordinary course of post.
In the present-day conception of official integrity the arrangement savours strongly of graft, but it was of a time
when government posts were considered desirable as much
for the opportunities for "pickings" as for their official remuneration, and fees and gratuities were recognised perquisites of the higher officials.

While the intelligence supplied by the correspondents was
the basis of the information published in *Lloyd's List* [1] it
was considered even more important that it should be made
available to those frequenting the Coffee House as *the* centre
of marine-insurance business. The rapid rise of Lloyd's was
largely due to the special facilities of this nature that were
provided.

The monopoly of shipping intelligence enjoyed by Lloyd's
Coffee House played an important part when the break came
in 1769, and Thomas Fielding, one of the waiters at Lloyd's,
set up the New Lloyd's in Pope's Head Alley. Before the
new enterprise could hope to succeed it was necessary to
break the monopoly, and to do this the co-operation of the
Post Office officials had to be obtained. How this was obtained is not clear although there was some acrimony between Thomas Lawrence, proprietor of the old Lloyd's, and
Fielding, his ex-waiter contemporary, of which there is evidence in advertisements in the press. It is clear, however,
that the monopoly of shipping intelligence supplied by the
correspondents and carried free by the Post Office was shared,
though it is not clear whether each of the parties obtained

[1] See pp. 8, 9.

information from the same correspondents or whether they carried on independently so far as the origin of the news was concerned.

These correspondents were not Lloyd's Agents, nor did they fulfil the functions of the Agents except in furnishing information, but undoubtedly they were the germ from which the agency system grew, although it was not until 1804 that further developments of any importance took place. In that year John Bennett, Jr., the first Secretary of Lloyd's, on his appointment as such, reorganised the intelligence service, opening up new channels of information and making contacts with persons at home and abroad who could furnish private and confidential information. The whole of the intelligence thus acquired was collated and to some extent edited by Bennett himself. Where previously it appears that all information received was published, now there seems to have been instituted some form of selection. Certain information which came to Lloyd's under the new system was of a confidential nature and as such was made available only to subscribers and those having access to the subscribers' rooms, but all intelligence which could properly be made public was and still is published. In so far as is possible Lloyd's has always freely furnished such information as can properly be made public. While the press is naturally required to pay for participating in the benefits of a service which involves enormous expenditure, individuals are frequently helped with gratuitous information, for instance, when a person inquires at Lloyd's for information as to the movements of a ship in which a friend or relative may be serving or travelling. After any major maritime disaster, such as the sinking of the *Titanic* or the torpedoing of the *Lusitania,* Lloyd's

freely gives to inquirers available information as to the names
of survivors or of those who have perished. In 1949, Lloyd's
set up an Information Department part of the duties of which
is to deal with such outside inquiries, and the usefulness of
this department is evident from the fact that it deals with an
average of 150 inquiries daily.

Lloyd's Agents are always ready to help anyone connected
with Lloyd's who calls upon their services. Such help is not
always of a technical nature. For instance, Lloyd's Agent at
Gothenburg was once approached by a member of Lloyd's
who wanted to know where, in Sweden, he could find a good
fishing district.

Duties of Agents

In the course of time, the duties and functions of Lloyd's
Agents have become very closely defined. It would be im-
possible within the scope of this work to give the instruc-
tions issued to Agents in full, but the following extract from
Lloyd's Calendar is an adequate summary of the duties of
Agents.

According to English law, the Master of a vessel has, as
Agent of the Shipowner, control over both ship and cargo,
and is responsible for both. Nothing less than a special power
can take away this control over the property confided to his
charge; but the Master can appoint an Agent, and it is presumed that he will, on behalf of the Assured or their representatives, readily avail himself of the assistance of an Agent
who is specially appointed by Lloyd's, and whose co-
operation and local knowledge will facilitate the settlement of
claims by the Underwriters. The Agent so appointed by the
Master is his representative, not the representative of the

Underwriters, but when a casualty is incurred, the interests of Shipowner, cargo owner and Underwriters became closely associated and what serves the interest of one will almost invariably serve the interests of all. In every act of interference, whether in an advisory capacity or otherwise, the Agent is not to be considered as the representative of the Underwriters upon any particular policy, unless he is specially instructed by such Underwriters so to act; but rather as a person whose duty it is, from the nature of his appointment, to protect Underwriters in general from fraud, negligence, needless expense or mismanagement, in the mode of treating property in peril or under average.

A provision in the Policy that, in case of damage, notice is to be given or application made to Lloyd's Agent, in order that he may survey the ship or goods or appoint a Surveyor for that purpose, does not constitute Lloyd's Agent the representative of the Underwriters on the particular Policy.

Unless he receives definite and specific instructions from Lloyd's, the authority of a Lloyd's Agent does not extend to accepting service on behalf of the Committee of the Corporation of Lloyd's or any Lloyd's underwriters, or to appearing for any of them before any Tribunal, or to taking any step which might be construed to be an admission by any of them of the jurisdiction of the tribunal. Immediately upon an Agent telegraphing to Lloyd's giving notice of a vessel being in distress in his district endeavours are made at Lloyd's to inform those interested in both ship and cargo and to obtain special instructions from the particular Underwriters concerned. The Agent is in no case empowered as the representative of the Underwriters to accept or reject abandonment of either ship or cargo; he should in such cases advise the persons who seek to abandon to communicate with their Underwriters.

In case of shipwreck the Agent will, in the absence of the Master or Owner or the legal guardians of the vessel or goods, take charge of the property and he will make such arrangements for its protection and preservation as he may consider expedient. He will also give immediate advice of the circumstances to the Assured, and follow their instructions in all cases where he can obtain them. In cases which require a technical knowledge of ships and/or their machinery, Lloyd's Agent is empowered, upon his own responsibility, to appoint a Surveyor well skilled in his profession.

In selecting a Surveyor for vessels and/or their machinery, where there is an exclusive Resident Officer of the London Salvage Association he should always be employed, if available, otherwise the Committee of Lloyd's would prefer, as a general rule, that the choice should fall upon the Surveyor of Lloyd's Register whenever there is one stationed in the Agency district (who will, in accordance with his instructions, sign as "Surveyor to Lloyd's Register"); the Agent must bear in mind, however, that he is responsible for the selection of the Surveyor, whoever he may be.

The Agent, in issuing the Report of the Surveyor he may select, should in every case authenticate the signature of the Surveyor on a special form drawn up for the purpose, to be attached to the Surveyor's report. When a vessel is in distress or on shore within the limits of his district, it is the duty of Lloyd's Agent to make such arrangements with the Master, should he or other parties interested request Lloyd's Agent's assistance, for recovering, saving or preserving the property as may be deemed expedient, and generally to assist the Master in any negotiations that may be necessary in this direction. It is repeated that the Agent, by this instruction, is not empowered as the representative of the underwriters to accept or reject abandonment of either ship or cargo; he should in such cases advise the persons who seek to abandon to communicate with their underwriters.

In all cases in which Lloyd's Agent has been requested to intervene where salvage or remuneration is claimed for assistance rendered to vessels, the Agent should attend the meetings of Commissioners, Magistrates, or other persons legally authorised to determine the amount, in order to rebut, by the evidence of the Master and Crew, any exaggerated statements on the part of the Salvors.

In cases where expensive and risky salvage operations are necessary, the Agent should always endeavour to procure from independent and responsible parties estimates for salving on the "no cure no pay" principle, at a percentage on the value saved.

Should any definite Contract on moderate terms not be procurable, the Agent should strenuously urge that the Agreement between Masters and Salvors with regard to remuneration should be on Lloyd's Form of Salvage Agreement and should recommend Masters to give preference to competent and adequately equipped Salvors who are prepared to contract on this basis.

The Agent when requested to survey goods which have suffered loss by damage or shortage shall always require the person requesting the survey to fill up and return to him the "Application for Survey" form. On his receiving the application for survey, the Agent should promptly make arrangements for an examination of the goods and he should impress on the consignees the necessity of taking delivery of their cargo at the earliest possible moment.

The Agent if called upon by the Consignee of cargo to hold a survey, will only act as sole surveyor when his own experience of the class of goods to be surveyed enables him to pronounce an accurate opinion; but when he does not act alone he will appoint a properly qualified Surveyor or Surveyors, whose signatures shall be authenticated by him. Surveys of cargoes, merely for the purpose of ascertaining if any or how many packages are damaged, are not within the ordinary duties of Lloyd's Agent, but may be undertaken by Lloyd's Agent if required by Merchants or Consignees, who should, however, be warned that, unless expressly provided for in the policy of insurance, the survey fees and other expenses incurred merely in the segregation of the damaged packages may not be recoverable from Underwriters as part of the expenses of proving a claim on the policy.

The Agent's remuneration must always be received from the parties employing him, or the owners of the property or their representatives, or out of the proceeds of what may be saved in cases of wreck.

When a Lloyd's Agent's services are employed, his charge should be made, not by a percentage on the value, but as a fee or reward proportioned by the time and trouble bestowed on the business. The Agent, should he consider such a course desirable, may demand a deposit of an amount not exceeding one guinea from a Consignee before proceeding to survey; this fee may be retained in case no certificate be granted.

No specific scale is laid down by the Committee of Lloyd's in respect of Surveyor's fees, as these probably depend upon the rates prevailing in the locality; but it is for the Agent to see that they are assessed on the same basis as those of the Agent himself—that is to say, according to the amount of time and trouble involved in connection with each particular case.

From the foregoing it will be seen that in laying down the instructions to Lloyd's Agents the Corporation has been very careful to ensure that, except under specific instructions from the underwriters concerned, an Agent is not to be considered or to act as the representative of the insurers or indeed as the active representative of the Corporation in so far as anything concerned with the ship, cargo, or other interest and the insurances thereon are concerned. Rather it is emphasised that while the Agent is appointed by the Corporation his employment with regard to any casualty or other matter concerning a ship, her cargo, or the insurance of either devolves upon him under instructions from some party. In the case of a ship this party would be the owner or his agent, possibly the Master. In the case of cargo the party issuing instructions to Lloyd's Agent might be the Master of the carrying ship, the consignee or his agent, the shipper or his agent, or the underwriters. It might even be some authority, such as a Dock and Harbour Board, or the Port Commissioners, who would instruct Lloyd's Agent with regard to some particular ship or interest. The point is that the Agent, while holding high status by reason of being appointed by Lloyd's, does not take the initiative in any arrangements with regard to a casualty or other happening except under specific instructions. This applies only in so far as any matter in which the shipowner or cargo owner or any other interested party requires assistance or advice. The Agent does take the initiative in obtaining information with regard to casualties, movement of ships, cargoes, or any other matter of interest to underwriters and in conveying such information to Lloyd's at the earliest possible moment. One of the functions of Lloyd's Agents to which special attention may be called is that of adjusting and settling claims under policies specifically authorising the settlement of claims payable abroad.

The Shipping Index and Other Publications

When Edward Lloyd inaugurated the practice of providing his customers with information concerning ships, including news of arrivals, departures, and casualties, he founded a system which was to develop into one of the most important of the services which the Corporation gives to its members and, in large part, to the world in general. Undoubtedly it was from the Coffee House practice of compiling lists of arrivals, departures, and casualties that the *Shipping Index* of today developed. This Index is, in its final form, a printed record of the latest reported movements of ocean-going tonnage, but before the reports reach this form they pass through several stages. Initially they emanate from Lloyd's Agents and Correspondents wherever they happen to be established, but they also include any information that may become available with regard to shipping movements, including that received from private sources, such as, for instance, news received by a shipowner or insurance broker and passed to the *Intelligence Department* at Lloyd's as an act of grace or for business purposes. The bulk of the reports, however, come from Agents and Correspondents. From these reports and from information from other sources the Index itself, today a card index of considerable size, is compiled. In this card index can be found a card for practically every ocean-going vessel, and while coasters are not supposed to be included, in practice quite a number of coasting vessels are indexed and have their particular cards. Each card has typewritten upon it the name of the ship, together with certain details, such as her tonnage, the year in which she was built, and the name of her owners. Then on the lines ruled on the card are entered the name of the port or place from which the report is received, the date on which the report is received, and the date of the issue of *Lloyd's List* in which the report is printed, together with the page on which the report appears. Arrivals are printed in black, sailings in red, and *paragraphs* in blue. A paragraph entry refers to any mention of the vessel concerned other than in the lists of arrivals and departures. Generally such entries refer to casualties, but not necessarily. Any mention of the ship's name is recorded in these paragraph entries with a very brief indication of the nature of the report, such as "ashore," "in collision," or "struck sunken wreck."

Work on the *Shipping Index* is continuous throughout the business day. A staff of clerks is employed entering the necessary details on the cards of the Index, and it is kept as closely up to the moment as is physically possible, the only time lag being that which is unavoidable in the preparing of the lists of details from which the entries are made.

The material from which the *Shipping Index* is compiled is also the material published, in normal times, in the columns of *Lloyd's List and Shipping Gazette,* a daily newspaper devoted to shipping movements and casualties. It is also embodied in a printed booklet issued daily, in which, in alphabetical order, the names of the ships in the Index are given with the latest report concerning each ship. Here also the name of the owner, tonnage, the year of build, and the current voyage are given so that the book is in effect a printed version of the latest entry against the name of every ship in the Index, and its title is, in fact, *Lloyd's Shipping Index.* The book is divided into three parts, of which the first, dealing with "Steamers, Motor Vessels, and Vessels with Auxiliary Power," is naturally the largest. The second part deals with "Miscellaneous Craft," such as tugs, cable vessels, dredgers, and training ships, and the third, and very attenuated part, deals with sailing vessels.[1] In normal times it is issued to subscribers who have signed a form stating that *Lloyd's Shipping Index* is required for their private use only and that in consideration of its being supplied they undertake not to permit its inspection by any person outside their office, nor to supply out-of-date copies to any persons outside their office. The penalty for breach of this undertaking is the cessation of the daily supply of a copy of the Index and the forfeiture of the subscription paid. *Lloyd's Shipping Index* and *Lloyd's List* are by no means the only publications issued by Lloyd's. There is *Lloyd's Shipping Index Weekly Supplement* having the same purpose as the Daily Index but on a weekly basis, *Lloyd's Loading List* giving the names of ships loading in British and Continental ports and their destinations and the names of the loading brokers, *Lloyd's Weekly Casualty Reports* summarising the casualty reports received during the week and published daily in *Lloyd's List*. *Lloyd's List Law Reports* deserve special mention. They contain reports of all shipping, commercial, and insurance cases of importance to shipping and insurance interests. Edited by a barrister they are more extensive than the reports which are published in *Lloyd's List*, and such has become their authority that they are now the reports generally cited in textbooks and other legal writings. They are supplemented by a *Digest* which summarises the cases in each 10 successive volumes and also serves as an index with cross references in addition to the

---

[1] The last sailing vessel disappeared from the Index in September, 1951.

indices of the separate issues which are made at the end of each law term and are embodied in annual volumes. *Lloyd's Calendar* is another important publication containing much detailed information on shipping and insurance matters. Among the various matters included are tide tables for over 70 ports; information on salvage plants and operations; foreign and colonial moneys; general and particular average; standard forms of policies; weights and measures; and nautical instruments.

LLOYD'S FORM OF SALVAGE AGREEMENT

One of the greatest services which Lloyd's has done the maritime world has been the promotion of *Lloyd's Form of Salvage Agreement* (see Fig. 5), the text of which appears on pages 149–157.

When a vessel is in distress it is of the utmost importance that assistance be rendered as quickly as possible and in the most efficient form.

Before the use of Lloyd's Form of Salvage Agreement became common ships and cargoes were sometimes lost, when they might have been saved, because the Master of the ship, or whoever was responsible for making arrangements for salvage, could not agree upon terms with potential salvors. Even where there was no deliberate intention to obtain an extortionate reward for undertaking operations of which the vessel in distress was in urgent need, delay sometimes occurred because a potential salvor hesitated to undertake operations which might involve him in considerable expenditure for which he had no guarantee of repayment.

The basis of Lloyd's Form of Salvage Agreement is that, by signing it, a salvor is guaranteed a proper remuneration

STANDARD FORM OF

SALVAGE AGREEMENT

(APPROVED AND PUBLISHED BY THE COMMITTEE OF LLOYD'S)

NO CURE—NO PAY.

On board the

Dated   19

It is HEREBY AGREED between Captain†   for and on
behalf of the Owners of the "   " her Cargo and
Freight and   for and on behalf of
(hereinafter called "the Contractor"*):—

† See Note 1 above

* See Note 2 above

** See Note 3 above

1. The Contractor agrees to use his best endeavours to salve the
and her cargo and take them into   or other place to be hereafter agreed with
the Master, providing at his own risk all proper steam and other assistance and labour. The
services shall be rendered and accepted as salvage services upon the principle of "no cure—no
pay" and the Contractor's remuneration in the event of success shall be **£   , unless
this sum shall afterwards be objected to as hereinafter mentioned in which case the remuneration
for the services rendered shall be fixed by Arbitration in London in the manner hereinafter
prescribed: and any other difference arising out of this Agreement or the operations thereunder
shall be referred to Arbitration in the same way. In the event of the services referred to in this
Agreement or any part of such services having been already rendered at the date of this Agreement
by the Contractor to the said vessel or her cargo it is agreed that the provisions of this Agreement
shall *mutatis mutandis* apply to such services.

2. The Contractor may make reasonable use of the vessel's gear anchors chains and other
appurtenances during and for the purpose of the operations free of costs but shall not unnecessarily
damage abandon or sacrifice the same or any other of the property.

3. Notwithstanding anything hereinbefore contained should the operations be only partially
successful without any negligence or want of ordinary skill and care on the part of the Contractor
or of any person by him employed in the operations, and any portion of the Vessel's Cargo or Stores
be salved by the Contractor, he shall be entitled to reasonable remuneration not exceeding a sum
equal to   per cent. of the estimated value of the property salved at
or if the property salved shall be sold there then not exceeding the like percentage of the net
proceeds of such sale after deducting all expenses and customs duties or other imposts paid or
incurred thereon but he shall not be entitled to any further remuneration reimbursement or
compensation whatsoever and such reasonable remuneration shall be fixed in case of difference by
Arbitration in manner hereinafter prescribed.

4. The Contractor shall immediately after the termination of the services or sooner notify
the Committee of Lloyd's of the amount for which he requires security to be given; and failing
any such notification by him not later than 48 hours (exclusive of Sundays or other days observed
as general holidays at Lloyd's) after the termination of the services he shall be deemed to require
security to be given for the sum named in Clause 1, or, if no sum be named in Clause 1, then for
such sum as the Committee of Lloyd's in their absolute discretion shall consider sufficient. Such
security shall be given in such manner and form as the Committee of Lloyd's in their absolute
discretion may consider sufficient but the Committee of Lloyd's shall not be in any way responsible
for the sufficiency (whether in amount or otherwise) of any security accepted by them nor for the
default or insolvency of any person firm or corporation giving the same.

5. Pending the completion of the security as aforesaid, the Contractor shall have a maritime
lien on the property salved for his remuneration. The salved property shall not without the consent
in writing of the Contractor be removed from   or
the place of safety to which the property is taken by the Contractor on the completion of the salvage
services until security has been given to the Committee of Lloyd's as aforesaid. The Contractor
agrees not to arrest or detain the property salved unless the security be not given within 14 days
(exclusive of Sundays or other days observed as general holidays at Lloyd's) of the termination of
the services (the Committee of Lloyd's not being responsible for the failure of the parties concerned
to provide the required security within the said 14 days) or the Contractor has reason to believe
that the removal of the property salved is contemplated contrary to the above agreement. In the
event of security not being provided as aforesaid or in the event of any attempt being made to

15-1-05
5-19-04
16-35-08
15-4-60

R 14

Fig. 5. Lloyd's form of salvage agreement. (For full text see
pp. 149–157.)

so that he can commence operations immediately the form
is signed without danger of any loss other than that which
is inevitable in the event of failure. Thus, at one stroke of
the pen, the delay, during which an insured interest imperilled by maritime disaster might deteriorate or even disappear, is avoided. The owners of the imperilled property
are protected against the ruinous bargains that might be
forced on them by avaricious salvors, while the salvors are
protected against the possibility of being unable to obtain
any reward that may become due to them on the completion
of their endeavours.

LLOYD'S

STANDARD FORM OF

SALVAGE AGREEMENT

(APPROVED AND PUBLISHED BY THE COMMITTEE OF LLOYD'S)

——————

NO CURE——NO PAY.

——————

On board the

Dated   19

It is hereby Agreed between Captain   for and on
behalf of the Owners of the "   " her Cargo and
Freight and   for and on behalf of
(hereinafter called "the Contractor") :—

1. The Contractor agrees to use his best endeavours to salve
the   and her cargo and take them into
or other place to be hereafter agreed with the Master, providing at his
own risk all proper steam and other assistance and labour. The services
shall be rendered and accepted as salvage services upon the principle
of "no cure—no pay" and the Contractor's remuneration in the event
of success shall be £   , unless this sum shall afterwards be
objected to as hereinafter mentioned in which case the remuneration
for the services rendered shall be fixed by Arbitration in London in the

manner hereinafter prescribed: and any other difference arising out of this Agreement or the operations thereunder shall be referred to Arbitration in the same way. In the event of the services referred to in this Agreement or any part of such services having been already rendered at the date of this Agreement by the Contractor to the said vessel or her cargo it is agreed that the provisions of this Agreement shall *mutatis mutandis* apply to such services.

2. The Contractor may make reasonable use of the vessel's gear anchors chains and other appurtenances during and for the purpose of the operations free of costs but shall not unnecessarily damage abandon or sacrifice the same or any other of the property.

3. Notwithstanding anything hereinbefore contained should the operations be only partially successful without any negligence or want of ordinary skill and care on the part of the Contractor or of any person by him employed in the operations, and any portion of the Vessel's Cargo or Stores be salved by the Contractor, he shall be entitled to reasonable remuneration not exceeding a sum equal to   per cent. of the estimated value of the property salved at or if the property salved shall be sold there then not exceeding the like percentage of the net proceeds of such sale after deducting all expenses and customs duties or other imposts paid or incurred thereon but he shall not be entitled to any further remuneration reimbursement or compensation whatsoever and such reasonable remuneration shall be fixed in case of difference by Arbitration in manner hereinafter prescribed.

4. The Contractor shall immediately after the termination of the services or sooner notify the Committee of Lloyd's of the amount for which he requires security to be given; and failing any such notification by him not later than 48 hours (exclusive of Sundays or other days observed as general holidays at Lloyd's) after the termination of the services he shall be deemed to require security to be given for the sum named in Clause 1, or, if no sum be named in Clause 1, then for such sum as the Committee of Lloyd's in their absolute discretion shall consider sufficient. Such security shall be given in such manner and form as the Committee of Lloyd's in their absolute discretion may consider sufficient but the Committee of Lloyd's shall not be in any way respon-

sible for the sufficiency (whether in amount or otherwise) of any security accepted by them nor for the default or insolvency of any person firm or corporation giving the same.

5. Pending the completion of the security as aforesaid, the Contractor shall have a maritime lien on the property salved for his remuneration. The salved property shall not without the consent in writing of the Contractor be removed from   or the place of safety to which the property is taken by the Contractor on the completion of the salvage services until security has been given to the Committee of Lloyd's as aforesaid. The Contractor agrees not to arrest or detain the property salved unless the security be not given within 14 days (exclusive of Sundays or other days observed as general holidays at Lloyd's) of the termination of the services (the Committee of Lloyd's not being responsible for the failure of the parties concerned to provide the required security within the said 14 days) or the Contractor has reason to believe that the removal of the property salved is contemplated contrary to the above agreement. In the event of security not being provided as aforesaid or in the event of any attempt being made to remove the property salved contrary to this agreement the Contractor may take steps to enforce his aforesaid lien. The Arbitrator or Arbitrators or Umpire (including the Committee of Lloyd's if they act in either capacity) appointed under Clauses 7 or 8 hereof shall have power in their absolute discretion to include in the amount awarded to the Contractor the whole or such part of the expenses incurred by the Contractor in enforcing his lien as they shall think fit.

6. After the expiry of 42 days from the date of the completion of the security the Committee of Lloyd's shall call upon the party or parties concerned to pay the amount thereof and in the event of nonpayment shall realize or enforce the security and pay over the amount thereof to the Contractor unless they shall meanwhile have received written notice of objection and a claim for Arbitration from any of the parties entitled and authorized to make such objection and claim or unless they shall themselves think fit to object and demand Arbitration. The receipt of the Contractor shall be a good discharge to the Committee of Lloyd's for any monies so paid and they shall incur no responsibility to any of the parties concerned by making such payment

and no objection or claim for Arbitration shall be entertained or acted upon unless received by the Committee of Lloyd's within the 42 days above mentioned.

7. In case of objection being made and Arbitration demanded the remuneration for the services shall be fixed by the Committee of Lloyd's as Arbitrators or at their option by an Arbitrator to be appointed by them unless they shall within 30 days from the date of this Agreement receive from the Contractor a written or telegraphic notice appointing an Arbitrator on his own behalf in which case such notice shall be communicated by them to the Owners of the vessel and they shall within 15 days from the receipt thereof give a written notice to the Committee of Lloyd's appointing another Arbitrator on behalf of all the parties interested in the property salved; and if the Owners shall fail to appoint an Arbitrator as aforesaid the Committee of Lloyd's shall appoint an Arbitrator on behalf of all the parties interested in the property salved or they may if they think fit direct that the Contractor's nominee shall act as sole Arbitrator; and thereupon the Arbitration shall be held in London by the Arbitrators or Arbitrator so appointed. If the Arbitrators cannot agree they shall forthwith notify the Committee of Lloyd's who shall thereupon either themselves act as Umpires or shall appoint some other person as Umpire. Any award of the Arbitrators or Arbitrator or Umpire shall (subject to appeal as provided in this Agreement) be final and binding on all the parties concerned and they or he shall have power to obtain call for receive and act upon any such oral or documentary evidence or information (whether the same be strictly admissible as evidence or not) as they or he may think fit, and to conduct the Arbitration in such manner in all respects as they or he may think fit, and to maintain reduce or increase the sum, if any, named in Clause 1, and shall if in their or his opinion the amount of the security demanded is excessive have power in their or his absolute discretion to condemn the Contractor in the whole or part of the expense of providing such security and to deduct the amount in which the Contractor is so condemned from the salvage remuneration. Unless the Arbitrators or Arbitrator or Umpire shall otherwise direct the parties shall be at liberty to adduce expert evidence on the Arbitration. The Arbitrators or Arbitrator and the Umpire (in-

cluding the Committee of Lloyd's if they act in either capacity) may charge such fees as they may think reasonable, and the Committee of Lloyd's may in any event charge a reasonable fee for their services in connection with the Arbitration, and all such fees shall be treated as part of the costs of the Arbitration and Award and shall be paid by such of the parties as the Award may direct. Interest at the rate of 5 per cent. per annum from the expiration of 14 days after the date of the publication of the Award by the Committee of Lloyd's until the date of payment to the Committee of Lloyd's shall (subject to appeal as provided in this Agreement) be payable to the Contractor upon the amount of any sum awarded after deduction of any sums paid on account. Save as aforesaid the statutory provisions as to Arbitration for the time being in force in England shall apply. The said Arbitration is hereinafter in this Agreement referred to as "the original Arbitration" and the Arbitrator or Arbitrators or Umpire thereat as "the original Arbitrator" or "the original Arbitrators" or "the Umpire" and the Award of such Arbitrator or Arbitrators or Umpire as "the original Award."

8. Any of the persons named under Clause 14 may appeal from the original Award by giving written Notice of Appeal to the Committee of Lloyd's within 14 days (exclusive of Sundays or other days observed as general holidays at Lloyd's) from the publication by the Committee of Lloyd's of the original Award; and any of the other persons named under Clause 14 may (without prejudice to their right of appeal under the first part of this clause) give written Notice of Cross-appeal to the Committee within 7 days after receipt by them of notice of such appeal. As soon as practicable after receipt of such notice or notices the Committee of Lloyd's shall themselves alone or jointly with another person or other persons appointed by them (unless they be the objectors) hear and determine the Appeal or if they shall see fit to do so or if they be the objectors they shall refer the Appeal to the hearing and determination of a person or persons selected by them. Any Award on Appeal shall be final and binding on all the parties concerned. No evidence other than the documents put in on the original Arbitration and the original Arbitrator's or original Arbitrators' and/or Umpire's notes and/or shorthand notes if any of the proceedings and oral evidence if any at the original Arbitration shall be used on the Appeal unless the

Arbitrator or Arbitrators on the Appeal shall in his or their discretion call for other evidence. The Arbitrator or Arbitrators on the Appeal may conduct the Arbitration on Appeal in such manner in all respects as he or they may think fit and may maintain increase or reduce the sum awarded by the original Award with the like power as is conferred by Clause 7 on the original Arbitrator or Arbitrators or Umpire to condemn the Contractor in the whole or part of the expense of providing security and to deduct the amount disallowed from the salvage remuneration. And he or they shall also make such order as they may think fit as to the payment of interest (at the rate of 5 per cent. per annum) on the sum awarded to the Contractor. The Arbitrator or Arbitrators on Appeal (including the Committee of Lloyd's if they act in that capacity) may direct in what manner the costs of the original Arbitration and of the Arbitration on Appeal shall be borne and paid and may charge such fees as they or he may think reasonable and the Committee of Lloyd's may in any event charge a reasonable fee for their services in connection with the Arbitration on Appeal and all such fees shall be treated as part of the costs of the Arbitration and Award on Appeal and shall be paid by such of the parties as the Award on Appeal shall direct. Save as aforesaid the statutory provisions as to Arbitration for the time being in force in England shall apply.

9. (a) In case of Arbitration if no notice of Appeal be received by the Committee of Lloyd's within 14 days after the publication by the Committee of the original Award the Committee shall call upon the party or parties concerned to pay the amount awarded and in the event of non-payment shall realize or enforce the security and pay therefrom to the Contractor (whose receipt shall be a good discharge to them) the amount awarded to him together with interest as hereinbefore provided.

(b) If notice of Appeal be received by the Committee of Lloyd's in accordance with the provisions of Clause 8 hereof they shall as soon as but not until the Award on Appeal has been published by them, call upon the party or parties concerned to pay the amount awarded and in the event of non-payment shall realize or enforce the security and pay therefrom to the

Contractor (whose receipt shall be a good discharge to them) the amount awarded to him together with interest if any in such manner as shall comply with the provisions of the Award on Appeal.

(c) If the Award on Appeal provides that the costs of the original Arbitration or of the Arbitration on Appeal or any party of such costs shall be borne by the Contractor, such costs may be deducted from the amount awarded before payment is made to the Contractor by the Committee of Lloyd's, unless satisfactory security is provided by the Contractor for the payment of such costs.

(d) Without prejudice to the provisions of Clause 4 hereof, the liability of the Committee of Lloyd's shall be limited in any event to the amount of security held by them.

10. The Committee of Lloyd's may in their discretion out of the security (which they may realize or enforce for that purpose) pay to the Contractor on account before the publication of the original Award and/or of the Award on Appeal such sum as they may think reasonable on account of any out-of-pocket expenses incurred by him in connection with the services.

11. The Master or other person signing this Agreement on behalf of the property to be salved is not authorized to make or give and the Contractor shall not demand or take any payment draft or order for or on account of the remuneration.

12. Any dispute between any of the parties interested in the property salved as to the proportions in which they are to provide the security or contribute to the sum awarded or as to any other such matter shall be referred to and determined by the Committee of Lloyd's or by some other person or persons appointed by the Committee whose decision shall be final and is to be complied with forthwith.

13. The Master or other person signing this Agreement on behalf of the property to be salved enters into this Agreement as Agent for the vessel her cargo and freight and the respective owners thereof and binds each (but not the one for the other or himself personally) to the due performance thereof.

14. Any of the following parties may object to the sum named in

Clause 1 as excessive or insufficient having regard to the services which proved to be necessary in performing the Agreement or to the value of the property salved at the completion of the operations and may claim Arbitration viz.:—(1) The Owners of the ship. (2) Such other persons together interested as Owners and/or Underwriters of any part not being less than one-fourth of the estimated value of the property salved as the Committee of Lloyd's in their absolute discretion may by reason of the substantial character of their interest or otherwise authorize to object. (3) The Contractor. (4) The Committee of Lloyd's —Any such objection and the original Award upon the Arbitration following thereon shall (subject to appeal as provided in this Agreement) be binding not only upon the objectors but upon all concerned, provided always that the Arbitrators or Arbitrator or Umpire may in case of objection by some only of the parties interested order the costs to be paid by the objectors only, provided also that if the Committee of Lloyd's be objectors they shall not themselves act as Arbitrators or Umpires.

15. If the parties to any such Arbitration or any of them desire to be heard or to adduce evidence at the original Arbitration they shall give notice to that effect to the Committee of Lloyd's and shall respectively nominate a person in the United Kingdom to represent them for all the purposes of the Arbitration and failing such notice and nomination being given the Arbitrators or Arbitrator or Umpire may proceed as if the parties failing to give the same had renounced their right to be heard or adduce evidence.

16. Any Award, notice, authority, order, or other document signed by the Chairman of Lloyd's or a Clerk to the Committee of Lloyd's on behalf of the Committee of Lloyd's shall be deemed to have been duly made or given by the Committee of Lloyd's and shall have the same force and effect in all respects as if it had been signed by every member of the Committee of Lloyd's.

For and on behalf of the Con-   For and on behalf of the Owners
tractor   of property to be salved

. . . .

(To be signed either by the Contractor personally or by the Master of the salving vessel or other person whose name is inserted in line 3 of this Agreement.)

(To be signed by the Master or other person whose name is inserted in line 1 of this Agreement.)

The form seems to owe its origin to what used to be a twofold scandal arising out of strandings on Kertch Bar. It appears that vessels frequently stranded on this bar in circumstances involving no serious danger. The first part of the scandal was that, when an unscrupulous shipowner knew that his vessel had incurred heavy weather or other damage for which underwriters would not be liable under the conditions of the policy, he would instruct his Captain to see that the vessel stranded on Kertch Bar, so that he could take advantage of the *Free of Average Warranty* of the policy under which claims of a certain nature are not payable "unless the vessel be stranded etc." The second part of the scandal was that the local salvage contractors formed a "ring" and would not undertake operations to refloat a stranded vessel except at extortionate prices although the vessel was in no particular danger. The most honest captain faced with the necessity of getting his vessel refloated often had to submit to such terms as the salvors chose to impose. Unless he did so his vessel might remain ashore indefinitely, losing freight and perhaps incurring penalties under the conditions of her charter. These extortionate claims fell partly upon underwriters and partly upon the mutual associations or *clubs* formed by shipowners for the purpose of bearing certain liabilities not covered by the marine policy. These clubs combined with Lloyd's and the marine-insurance companies in a movement which initially was intended to deal with strandings in the Black Sea and the Dardanelles, and, in fact, operated largely within those limitations up to the early 1890's. At that time, in conjunction with a proposal to create a salvage company of paramount importance, in which Lloyd's, The Salvage Association, the Liverpool Salvage Association, and the marine-insurance companies should combine, efforts were made to extend the field in which Lloyd's Form of Salvage Agreement operated. The former proposal came to naught, but the campaign for the more widespread use of Lloyd's Form made headway until it became what it is today, almost universally accepted throughout the maritime world. It has been amended from time to time, the most important amendment being in 1926 when provision was made for appeals from any initial awards, the most recent amendment being in 1950 when provision was made for "cross appeals" and certain textual emendations were also made.

Lloyd's Form of Salvage Agreement is on the *no-cure-no-pay* basis. It provides for the payment of a stated sum as the salvor's remuneration in the event of success, but the essential feature of the agreement is to be found in the provision that

> Unless this sum shall afterwards be objected to as hereinafter mentioned in which case the remuneration . . . shall be fixed by Arbitration in London in the manner hereinafter prescribed.

Arbitration

In the event of any objection to the proposed sum of remuneration, it is open to the contractor to appoint an *arbitrator* on his behalf, in which case the managing owner of the ship may also appoint an arbitrator. If an objection is made, and the salvor does not appoint an arbitrator, the

Committee of Lloyd's may act as arbitrators or may appoint an arbitrator. If both parties have appointed an arbitrator and the two arbitrators cannot agree the Committee of Lloyd's either themselves, or by a person appointed by them, act as umpire. Any properly interested party to the contract may appeal against any award, and in the event of an appeal being lodged, the Committee of Lloyd's may, alone or jointly with another person or persons appointed by them, determine the appeal, or they may refer the whole matter to a person appointed by them. In practice it is customary to refer both awards and appeal to eminent lawyers with experience of maritime matters, the appointments being made from a roster which includes the names of some of the leading barristers who practice in maritime law. This is, of course, only a broad outline of the provisions of the agreement embodied in the form which also provides for the safeguarding of the interests of the parties, especially with regard to the giving of security, where required, for the ultimate payment of the salvor's remuneration, the salvor agreeing, in return for this undertaking, not to arrest the ship or the property salved.

Collision Cases

In July, 1933, Lloyd's also promoted a form of agreement for use in collision cases, the intention being to avoid litigation over the question of blame and to prevent vessels which have been in collision from being arrested as security for alleged damages. The agreement is admittedly not suitable for every case of collision, and it has not obtained the widespread use that the salvage agreement has, but it has proved beneficial in limiting litigation and in promoting the use of the cheaper and less tedious means of settling disputes by arbitration. It is similar to the salvage agreement in the matter of appointing arbitrators and in the provisions with regard to appeals.

LLOYD'S POLICY SIGNING OFFICE

Elsewhere in this work, reference is made to the system, now almost peculiar to Lloyd's, by which the formal and final acceptance of a risk is completed by the affixing of the names of the underwriters to the policy. Initially each underwriter actually signed the policy, against the amount of his *line*. When the group or Syndicate system was developed it became necessary to empower some individual to sign for the several underwriters composing each group, and towards the end of the nineteenth century the use of rubber stamps by means of which the names of the underwriters were imprinted on the policy greatly facilitated the process of completing the document. The person empowered to sign on behalf of a group or Syndicate was not necessarily an important official. Indeed he was customarily a junior, for the work was largely of a routine nature and consisted of filling in the amount of the line written on the risk against the names of the underwriters and appending the amount written in abbreviated terms together with the signature of the person entrusted with the operation. The process of completing a policy by this method was tedious and wasteful of time and clerical labour. A broker's clerk had to carry a policy to the Box of each underwriter on the risk, in rotation, fetching it from the Box of the first underwriter to whom the policy was submitted for signature and taking it to the Box of the next underwriter, this process being repeated until all the underwriters on the risk had signed the policy. The system also had the disadvantage of subjecting the policy to much wear and tear. An important policy for a large amount would often be soiled and blotted, sometimes even torn, before it was completed, and sometimes policies were lost during their passage from one underwriter's Box to that of another. Indeed there used to be a special drawer reserved for lost policies under the control of the Superintendent of The Room, and the first thing a broker's clerk would do, if a policy was missing, was to search this drawer. This process added further to the wear and tear on policies, but it continued, largely because of the inertia of the underwriters and brokers, until 1916.

In that year, consequent upon the recruitment of the younger men of the nation to serve in the Army, a grave shortage of junior clerical workers brought about what was then considered to be a wartime emergency measure, and *Lloyd's Policy Bureau*, as it was then called, was created to sign policies on a collective basis. The matter was finally arranged at a meeting of the Committee of Lloyd's in 1916 when Mr. (now Sir) Walter Hargreaves, of the brokerage firm of C. T. Bowring & Co. (Insurance) Ltd., volunteered to draw up a scheme for facilitating the signing of policies. Owing to the shortage of junior male labour it was evident that the solution of the problem would have to be sought by the employment of girls. In those days female labour in City offices was almost entirely composed of typists, and there was not even a nucleus of girls with any experience of policy drafting, clauses, or the general details of marine-insurance business. A large staff of girls was, however, recruited and housed in offices in Great Winchester Street, not far from the Royal Exchange, where Lloyd's was then situated. The fundamen-

tal idea was that a policy should be left at this office and that
the girls should affix the necessary signatures by means of
rubber stamps similar to those previously used by the underwriters' own clerks. This would do away with the necessity
for hawking a policy from Box to Box in The Room. The process would be virtually the same, but it would be condensed
so that, where previously a policy had to be taken from Box
to Box, gaining the signature of one Syndicate at each, it
would be dealt with in one operation in one place.

The chief difficulty in the initial stages of the scheme was
that its operation required a knowledge of the initials used
by underwriters as their symbol of acceptance of a risk. This
difficulty was aggravated by the fact that some underwriters
used initials that were traditional and that, even where an
underwriter used his own initials, they assumed an illegible
character in the nature of a business hieroglyphic, rather than
any calligraphic reproduction of alphabetical letters. It is
on record that when the new system was being inaugurated
one of the girls asked, "Can you tell me what the croquet
hoop means on this slip"? It was the initial of a well-known
underwriter of that period, C. I. de Rougemont.

Policy Checking

The organisation of Lloyd's Underwriters' Signing Bureau
(now Policy Signing Office) was, however, so sound, and
those entrusted with its higher administration were so able,
that it quickly got into its stride and undoubtedly has proved
a most efficient labour-saving device. One of its great advantages is that in ensures the uniform checking of policies by
experts. When policies were signed individually at the Boxes
of underwriters, the *signing clerk* of each underwriter was

supposed to check the policy against the slip, to ensure that the clauses and conditions of the contract conformed with those agreed upon between broker and underwriter when the risk was written. In practice it was usually only the signing clerk of the leading underwriter, the underwriter whose initial was first on the slip, who checked the policy. If the signing clerks of the other underwriters on the risk saw that the policy had been signed by the clerk of the leading underwriter, they would assume it to be in order and would sign the policy without first checking it. Here it should be noted that, while the Lloyd's Underwriters' Signing Bureau was initially set up as an expedient of the First World War, it proved so efficient for all its purposes that it was retained as a permanent organisation of the market at Lloyd's and was given the name of Lloyd's Policy Signing Office in 1928, although from force of habit some Lloyd's men still refer to it as "The Bureau."

When the Signing Bureau was set up, experienced clerks were employed to do the checking, and since this was their only task and they were not concerned in entering the details of the risk, signing the policy, working out the premium, etc., a very high degree of efficiency was attained. Indeed, it has been said that the checking is too meticulous and that policies are sometimes delayed in the process of signing because the checkers have queried some quite immaterial discrepancy between the terms and conditions of the slip and those of the policy, but there can be no doubt that this scrupulous insistence on exactitude makes for efficiency and prevents misunderstandings and disputes. The affixing of the stamp of an underwriter's Names, with the amount of his line, or its wartime equivalent noted below, completes a policy, but, under the system of the Policy Signing Office, a further process is required. In every Lloyd's policy there is a space in which the official seal of the Policy Signing Office is embossed, and no policy submitted to the Office is valid unless, in addition to the impress of the underwriters' Name stamps and the filling in of the amounts underwritten by each Syndicate, the seal is embossed thereon.

Records

So much for the actual process of signing policies; the system of the Policy Signing Office also entails the keeping of records of policies signed on behalf of the underwriters. These records are the basis of the particulars which are furnished daily to the underwriters in the form of *advice cards* containing information in respect of each risk, signed, including the line or amount underwritten and the premium, and supported by an accounting tabulation. It is from these cards that he makes the necessary entries for accounting between himself and the brokers with whom he does business. Another function of the Office is the settlement of returns of premium, as in the case of a ship that has been laid up in port during the currency of the policy for a period of 30 days, this being a method of adjusting the premium to the decreased risk during the period in which the vessel has not been exposed to the full perils of ocean navigation.

Another wartime development already referred to which may prove permanent is the printing, on every Lloyd's policy, of every Syndicate of underwriters transacting business at Lloyd's. When a policy is presented for signature, the amounts underwritten by the Syndicates on the risk are filled in, and the official number of each of these Syndicates is stamped on the policy in an appointed place. The other Syndicates remain, as it were, dormant. Their names are printed on the policy but have no amounts entered against them, and their official numbers are not stamped on the policy in the appointed place. By this means, the process of stamping policies with the names of individual Syndicates is eliminated, and much time and labour is saved.

THE CLAIMS OFFICE

In 1917, as an adjunct of the Signing Bureau, a "claims-settling bureau" was set up, the title of which was subsequently changed to *Lloyd's Underwriters' Claims Office*. It is not yet operating for every Syndicate at Lloyd's, some still maintaining their own claims-settling organisations, but a very large proportion of the Syndicates are members of the Office, and it seems probable that in the course of time it will become the generally accepted channel through which claims on Lloyd's policies are settled.

At present it is passing through a process of evolution, and its importance and its functions are growing every year as more and more Syndicates come within its orbit. Nevertheless some underwriters still retain a considerable amount of control over the settlement of their claims. In other cases the Office is empowered to deal with claims direct, and the first intimation that an underwriter receives that a claim has been settled on his behalf may be the submission of the details in the daily record of settlements that is submitted to him by the Office.

The Office also maintains a very close liaison with Lloyd's Average Department [1] which deals with recoveries of gen-

[1] See pp. 166–169.

eral-average deposits and salvages. The Office is also represented, through its principal official, at the weekly meetings of claims adjusters of Lloyd's and the marine-insurance companies which is an important feature of the organisation of the London market. At these meetings current problems, either general or relating to specific claims, are discussed, and when occasion requires, decisions as to co-operative action are taken. It follows that, since the Office represents a considerable number of Syndicates at Lloyd's, its participation in these meetings through its principal official is most advantageous.

Claims Payable Abroad and the Average Department

Among the more important services rendered to members of Lloyd's by the Corporation is the settlement of claims abroad. The principle of the service is very simple. If a merchant or shipper wants to be able to collect at some foreign port any claim that may be incurred on a policy, a special policy form is used bearing a provision reading:

> This is to certify that Lloyd's Agent at the port of........
> has been authorised to adjust and settle on behalf of the
> Underwriters and to purchase on behalf of the Corporation of
> Lloyd's in accordance with the Standing Regulations for the
> Settlement of Claims abroad, any claim which may arise on
> this policy, and that a fee of .... has been paid to
> me for that purpose.
> ....For the Committee of
> Lloyd's

The name of the port at which claims are to be settled and the fee paid for the service are inserted in the appropriate place. The policy is then taken to Lloyd's by the broker who has placed the risk and is registered there. Signature by an official of the Corporation completes this endorsement. The policy also embodies the following provision:

Lloyd's Agent at the port of . . . . is authorised to adjust and settle all claims on this Policy, and claims are payable in accordance with such adjustment and settlement as provided by Lloyd's Standing Regulations for the Settlement of Claims Abroad, all of which shall be considered as part of this Policy, but the Agent is not personally responsible and has no authority to represent the Underwriters or the Corporation of Lloyd's or the Committee of Lloyd's in any legal proceedings.

It is mutually agreed that in accordance with the aforesaid Regulations, the benefit of this Policy, and the right to receive or endorse over claims thereon, may be passed, whether before or after the claim, by endorsement, and that such endorsee or the bearer of the Policy, if endorsed in blank, on production of this Policy, shall have power to receive and give receipts for, or to endorse or assign over, as provided by the said Regulations, any claim thereon. All disputes must be referred to England for settlement, and no legal proceedings shall be taken to enforce any claim except in England where the Underwriters are alone domiciled and carry on business.

It is further agreed that in accordance with the aforesaid Regulations the Underwriters shall pay the remuneration to Lloyd's Agent for adjusting and settling any claim on this Policy on the basis of the percentage specified in such Regulations and that the same shall be paid by them to the Corporation of Lloyd's for remittance to the Agent.

It will be seen that the fee paid on registration of the policy at Lloyd's does not cover the cost of adjustment, which naturally varies with the amount of the claim; the percentage of the claim, which is the basis of the remuneration of Lloyd's Agent, affords a satisfactory means of payment.

The practice of settling claims abroad dates back to about 1885 and was operated first in conjunction with the Communications Department, which in those days maintained the duties of instructing Lloyd's Agents on behalf of underwriters and generally of carrying on liaison between the Corporation and Agents. About ten years later the system of collecting and distributing to underwriters refunds of general-average deposits and salvages was instituted and was undertaken by the staff who attended to the settlement-of-claims-abroad organisation. At this time the organisation was an integral part of the Secretary's office. The Communications Department had no system of collecting and coordinating information about claims. If a Lloyd's Agent asked for instructions with regard to any particular casualty, a clerk from the Secretary's office would go into the Underwriting Room and endeavour to discover the interested underwriters. Sometimes it was necessary to find out who were the interested underwriters by posting a notice on the Notice Board asking them to communicate with the Secretary's office. Having identified the leading underwriter on the risk, the clerk would ask him for his instructions, and it says much for the confidence reposed in Lloyd's Agents that these were frequently that the Agents should act for the interests of all concerned as if the ship or goods were uninsured. The same machinery used for the payment of claims abroad and the recovery of general-average deposits and salvages was also used for the conveyance to underwriters of information of a confidential nature. This organisa-

tion eventually became the *Average Department,* which, today, functions in many ways over and above the primary
duties of organising the settlement of claims abroad. It is
significant of the close collaboration of Lloyd's with the
marine-insurance companies that the Department's services
are as much at the disposal of the companies as of Lloyd's
Underwriters, and are freely used by them.

THE SALVAGE ASSOCIATION

One of the most important adjuncts of the marine-insurance
market is *The Salvage Association,* an organisation the creation of which was inevitable when the growth of the English marine-insurance market reached a stage at which joint
action between the various units became more and more
difficult owing to the increasing number of insurers. When
the market was comprised solely of Lloyd's and the two
monopolistic corporations, The London Assurance and the
Royal Exchange Assurance, joint action was easy, but after
the repeal of the monopoly in 1824, the steady increase in
the number of reputable insurance companies made co-
operation without some central organisation cumbersome.
In 1856 a General Meeting of Lloyd's approved the formation of The Salvage Association, voted £500 as a grant in
aid, and provided temporary offices for the accommodation
of the new organisation. The London Assurance, Royal
Exchange, Alliance, Indemnity Mutual, and the marine-insurance companies also contributed £200 apiece; 175 members of Lloyd's contributed 5 guineas each, and the Royal
Mail Steam Packet Company contributed 10 guineas. The
composition of this list of subscribers is interesting. The
Alliance and the Indemnity companies were the two first in

the field when the monopoly was broken, and the Marine
was established in 1836; in 1856 there were a considerable
number of marine companies. The fact that the initial subscription was limited to the oldest component units of the
market suggests that they, and they only, operated in close
collaboration with Lloyd's which was still the leading organisation and whence the initiative in reforms seems to
have come without exception until the creation of the Institute of London Underwriters in 1884. The fact that only
one shipowning concern, albeit an important one, partici-
pated in the creation of The Salvage Association is curious.
That such participation was contemplated from the first is
evident from the original constitution of the Association.

In addition to their initial subscriptions, each contributing
party agreed to make up any deficiency in the income of
the Association by payments pro rata of their original subscriptions, but the success of the undertaking made it unnecessary to make any calls on the guarantors although Lloyd's
voted a second grant of £500 in 1861. In 1867 it was incorporated by Royal Charter, the Charter embodying the original rules and regulations.

The long title of the Association is The Association for
the Protection of Commercial Interests as Respects Wrecked
and Damaged Property. This name really describes its activities more accurately than its short title because the
Association has never undertaken salvage in the sense of an
operative salvage company, although at one time it owned
pumps and other plant that were at the disposal of tug
owners and others who undertook salvage operations on the
instructions of the Association.

Operation

The fundamental basis of the constitution of the Association is the protection of commercial interests, and while from the nature of its organisation it operates almost if not entirely in the interests of underwriters, those interests are so closely associated with the interests of the assured that the Association does, in fact, fulfil the duty of protecting commerce in general. From the outset the Association has operated in very close collaboration with Lloyd's agency system which has in a very large measure contributed to its efficiency and success. The primary objects of the Association, according to the Rules, are "the investigating by all lawful means of frauds practiced or attempted or intended to be practiced with respect to vessels and their cargoes" and "to take all lawful means of punishing the offenders."

The Association operates largely by taking charge of the negotiations concerning casualties in which underwriters are interested. When any such casualty is reported it is a very common practice for underwriters, on receiving formal notice of a pending claim, to instruct the Salvage Association to act on their behalf. Thence onward the Association takes all the steps necessary to protect and preserve the insured property, be it ship or cargo. Initially it operated through ships' captains and other nautical surveyors, men of considerable practical experience but without the technical training of shipwrights or engineers. With the development of the steamship it became necessary to obtain the services of men with the requisite technical equipment, and trained experts were added to the staff on a salaried basis although the system of employing surveyors who were paid only for the actual work done continued and still continues. In the course of time it was found necessary to widen the scope of the Association's organisation, and salaried surveyors were established in the outports (Liverpool, Glasgow, etc.) and in the United States and Canada. Until the war intervened the Association had offices in Belgium and Holland which have been reinstated since those countries were liberated.

The broad lines on which the Association operates are that, when instructed by underwriters to take charge of their interests, they instruct the most readily available surveyor to inspect the damaged interests, after which the Association takes action in accordance with his reports. Now that the Association no longer owns any plant, it negotiates with the best available concern qualified to undertake the work required. One of its most important functions is to arrange, where necessary, for salvage to be undertaken at a fixed remuneration, rather than on the salvage basis under which the salvors' remuneration is dependent largely on the value of the property salved. In simple cases where failure is very unlikely it is generally possible to make a contract with a salvage concern for a fixed sum. The amount is generally less than that which would have to be paid if the salvor were to receive a reward only in the event of success, and failure on his part would mean that he bore the cost of fruitless operations without any claim against the owners or insurers of the property. Such is the standing of the Association that its contracts are accepted without question by contractors all over the world, and shipowners and others concerned in any casualty in respect of which the Association is instructed gladly co-operate with its officers. Its management is vested in a committee elected annually and composed of members of Lloyd's and representatives of the marine-insurance market. A period of office on the Committee is generally regarded as a hall mark of an underwriter's standing in the market.

The Association is not, primarily, a profit-making concern, its object being to serve the interests of underwriters by minimising their losses, but by 1925 its accumulated funds had reached a total of £102,000, and before the war its annual turnover was between £1,250,000 and £1,500,000. Its income is derived largely from charges for services rendered.

During wartime the activities of the Association are increased in both measure and importance, and during the First World War it played a very material role in salving both ships and vessels damaged by enemy action. During the Second World War its importance was even greater than during the first for it organised a special department for dealing with claims on cargo insured against marine risks in the open market on behalf of the Ministries of Food and Supply, and also had special functions in relation to the tonnage from the overrun countries of Europe that had come under British control.

While the primary object of the Association is to protect the interests of underwriters in so far as they are affected by maritime perils, it also serves another very important purpose in providing underwriters with material upon which they can formulate their business policy. For instance, the Association is able, through its manifold contacts at repairing ports, to compile very important statistics on the cost of ship repairs, the extent of theft and pilferage at docks, and similar matters, and to make this information available to underwriters.

Through the nature of its operations, the Association is also largely instrumental in detecting and preventing fraudulent claims on insurance policies, and during the epidemic of fraudulent castings away which resulted from the shipping slump after the First World War, it dealt with, on behalf of underwriters, 63 cases of Greek vessels involving insured values aggregating £3,847,832 and 21 Spanish vessels with aggregate values of £1,879,800. It says much for the care with which the Association handled the difficult and delicate investigations necessary to the detection of these frauds that in no case in which underwriters resisted a claim on the grounds that it was fraudulent were they unsuccessful in the courts.

LLOYD'S REGISTER

"A1 at Lloyd's," or more briefly, "A1" is a term in common use as a synonym of excellence throughout the English-speaking world and is used by millions who have no idea that the term is a technical one used, in shipping, to denote a ship entirely staunch and seaworthy with her rigging and gear in perfect condition. How that term came into use in the first place must be a matter of conjecture because the origin of ship classification is obscure. It is believed that during the early part of the eighteenth century individual underwriters and merchants maintained their own ship registers, *i.e.*, records compiled from such data as were available with regard to the condition of the ships they insured and in which their cargoes were carried.

The Merchant would not be willing to employ, nor the Underwriter to insure, a ship, without first acquainting himself with her fitness for the carriage of merchandise across the Sea (*Annals of Lloyd's Register*).

In all probability records in the nature of a ship register were kept at the original Lloyd's Coffee House, though none seems to have survived. Colour is lent to this theory by the fact that the first printed ship register does not seem to have been hailed as something new or to have been the subject of any public appeal for subscribers. It was issued in 1760 and cannot, as The Annals of Lloyd's Register says,

have sprung Minerva-like, complete in all its parts, except as the result of a long time spent in collecting and arranging the detailed particulars of so large a number of vessels, many of which had already been inspected and reported upon by Surveyors.

That no copies of any earlier registers, either in manuscript or in print, have been found is not surprising. The fire which destroyed the Royal Exchange in 1838 destroyed at the same time many irreplaceable records, amongst them the files of early *Lloyd's Lists*, and it is probable that if any old Registers were preserved they were at Lloyd's and perished in the fire. The fire may also be responsible for the fact that the oldest extant printed Register is not that of 1760, but bears the date 1764–1765–1766. It is in the library of Lloyd's Register of Shipping in Fenchurch Street, London, and contains the embryo of the current system of keeping the Register up to date by having three columns, headed 64, 65, and 66, respectively. The column headed 64, being that for the year of issue, has the class of the vessels printed; in the column headed 65 a few printed classifications are intermingled with manuscript entries, and in the column headed 66 all the entries are in manuscript. It is clear that underwriters were supplied with details of successive surveys from year to year and were able to keep their registers up to date by adding, in manuscript, the details of each successive classification.

Early Registers

The Register of 1764 has 13 columns in all, headed respectively "Former"; "Present"; "Master"; "Port"; "to Port"; "Tons"; "Guns"; "M"; "Built and Year"; "Owners"; "64"; "65"; "66." "Former" is the column in which, if a vessel had changed her name, her previous name was entered. Under "Present," the present name of the ship appeared. "Master" headed the column in which the name of the captain was given. "Port" was the vessel's home port, and "to Port" headed the column showing the vessel's accustomed trade. "Tons" gave the vessel's tonnage, and "Guns" the number of guns, but this column was used in practice for annotations of structural details, as, for instance, "SdB," indicating a single deck with a tier of beams. Under "Built and Year" appeared the port of construction and the year in which the vessel was built. Her owner's name appeared in the next column, and then, under the column headings "64," "65," and "66," the ship's class, as it would now be known.

In this early Register capital letters were used. The vowels indicated the condition of the hull, while the letters "G," "M," and "B" applied to her rigging, the latter signifying "Good," "Middling," and "Bad," respectively. The vowels took their alphabetical sequence so that "A" meant a ship whose hull was in perfect condition, seaworthy, and staunch for her accustomed trade. In a page of this Register, reproduced in The Annals of Lloyd's Register, only two vessels earn the highest classification. The *Eagle* of Belfast, built in 1864 and therefore quite new, is classed "AG" and so is the *Earl of Sandwich,* built at Hull in 1762. It is noticeable that the *Earl of Sandwich,* another vessel of the same name and tonnage built at Yarmouth in the same year, is classed only "EM," that is to say, her hull was not in perfect condition and her gear was only "Middling."

The next Register, in point of date, preserved in the library of Lloyd's Register, is dated 1768–1769, and one is led to speculate whether there was, in fact, a Register for 1767, or whether underwriters continued the one for 1764–1765 and 1766 by adding the data for 1767 in the margin. The argument against this is that the extant copy does not seem to have any marginal notes for 1767. The argument for it is that the 1768 Register has columns for 4 years in all, two being annotated in print, and two being left blank for manuscript annotation. The layout is entirely different. The columns are not headed. In the first are consecutive numbers, presumably index numbers, perhaps the forerunners of present-day Registered Numbers. In the second column is the name of the ship with, for the first time, indication of her rig, as for instance, "S" for ship, "Bg" for brig. In the third column appears the name of the master, and in the fourth, tonnage and structural details: "SD" for single deck, etc. A fifth narrow column is blank, and in the sixth the port of building is given, as well as the year of construction. The seventh column shows the ownership, and then come two columns of printed classification, followed by a column in which the vessel's trade is shown, for example, "Pool N. York." The last two columns are for manuscript annotations of class.

The outstanding feature of this Register is the change in the symbols of classification. In place of vowels in capital letters, small letters in alphabetical sequence are used, "a," "b," and "c," while large numerals take the place of the "G," "M," and "B" for indicating the condition of gear and rigging. Thus "ª1" denotes a first-class ship with perfect gear and rigging, "ᵇ2" would be a ship not too well kept up with rather indifferent rigging, and so on.

The third Register preserved at Lloyd's Register is dated 1775–1776, and again there is no accounting for the hiatus, though in all probability there was a Register for 1772–1774. It is in this Register for 1775 that the symbol "A1" appears. Again the characters used for classification had been changed, and once more the vowels, in capitals, denoted the class of the ship and numerals the class of the rigging. This system continued, and continues with modifications, to the present day. The reason for this settled practice can probably be found in the fact that while the earlier Registers, those for 1760 to 1769, were compiled in the Lombard Street Coffee-House days, Angerstein and his fellow underwriters removed in 1769 to the "New Lloyd's" in Pope's Head Alley and subsequently to the Royal Exchange, and Lloyd's became an Association with a Constitution, rather than a mere community with a common meeting place and no great measure of organised existence.

Some idea of the manner in which classification was carried out in the early days of Registers has come down to us

through Park's *System of the Law of Marine Insurance,*
published in 1769. In this work there is reference to an un-
seaworthiness case over the *Mills,* a frigate, the relevant passage reading:

> George Hayley Esq. the first Underwriter of this policy and
> many other persons by whom policies of insurance are gen-
> erally underwritten, keep a Register in which all ships usually
> insured by them are entered with an account of the age, con-
> struction and visible goodness of the vessels and to whom
> they belong, and also employ a Surveyor whose business it
> is to survey such ships; that the ship in question at the time of
> underwriting the policy and long before, had been entered in
> such Register; and previous to her last outward bound voyage
> had been surveyed by one Thomas Whitewood who was
> then employed by the said George Hayley and other Under-
> writers as such Surveyor; and, as far as appeared to the said
> Thomas Whitewood, was in good condition and perfectly fit
> to undertake a voyage to and from the Leeward Islands, but
> the Surveyor did not, neither could he, examine the bolts and
> spikes for the reasons aforesaid, but did survey, as far as is
> ever practiced in such cases. . . .

This series of Registers commencing in 1760 was known
as the *Green Book* (or *Underwriters Book*) from the colour
of the binding, and green has always been the colour in
which many Lloyd's books are bound. The portrait of John
Bennett, Jr., first Secretary of Lloyd's, shows a volume
bound in green with the criss-cross inlaid ornamentation
round the edges, which corresponds exactly with the binding on the *Casualty Book* of today. So far as is known, though
there is no precise evidence, the Green Book was supported
exclusively by underwriters for the sole use of the subscribers,

whose subscriptions formed the only source of revenue.

Apparently the confidential nature of the Register was not at first preserved with any strictness, for in the volume for 1889–1890 there are by-laws calling attention to the fact that the interest of the society was

> greatly hurt by the custom of shewing the Books, and leaving them in Places where they are but too common, thereby preventing many Underwriters from becoming Members, who, though they reap the Advantages and Benefits in common with them, do not pay their Quota towards the expenses of the institution, thereby, as much as in them lies, reducing the Members to the Necessity of paying larger Subscriptions.

The by-laws go on to lay down that if any member shall

> shew or give his Book to any Person whatever, not a Member of the Society, to read the Description or Character therein of any Ship, or shall read the same to him, or tell him the same after looking at the Book, such Member shall forfeit the Sum of 5s. 3d. and for the second Breach of this by-law the Sum of 10s. 6d., for the third Breach thereof the sum of £1. 1. 0. and for the fourth (all of them in Manner aforesaid and within the Year) his book shall not be posted any more, except he pays the sum of Two Guineas and all former Forfeitures, within Fourteen Days of the Notice he shall receive thereof from the Secretary, or pays the sum of Five Guineas for a new Book any time thereafter, within the Year, and delivers up his old one.

A further by-law lays down a forfeit "in like Manner as before, for the 1st, 2nd, 3rd and 4th Breach" if the book is left in any place, "except where the member shall himself appoint constantly to leave the same locked up" or if the book be found in the possession of any person not a member, while for the entire loss of the book the forfeit "shall be settled by the Committee, and the Member be obliged to pay Five Guineas for a new one."

The next development in the Green Book seems to have been in the issue of 1797–1798, in which the symbols were again changed, this time to "M" for first class, "G" for second class, and "L" for third class, with two lower but rarely used classes of "Q" and "Z," and the numerals attaching to rigging and equipment were changed to 8 or 4. At the same time, the principle of classification was changed so as to depend entirely on the age of the vessel and the place where she was built. For instance, a vessel built on the Thames would be considered first class for 13 years, but another of the same type built in a northern port would hold her first class for only 8 years. While this does not seem to have been entirely equitable, it is beyond doubt that London-built ships of that period were, in fact, superior to those built at most if not all the outports.

This change in the principle of classification caused strong feeling among shipowners who made strong representations on the matter. Having failed to secure any redress, London shipowners, who might have been thought unduly favoured by the new system, made arrangements to set up their own Register. This was first published in 1799, and from the colour of its binding came to be known as the *Red Book*.

Now it was the shipowners' turn to use the capital vowels and numerals for classification purposes, the Red Book having A1 for Thames-built ships, if entirely of British oak and well fastened, for a period of 12 years, while ships built in the outports on the same conditions, were classed A1 for 10 years. The second class "E" covered all ships kept in perfect repair and without apparent defects, being calculated to carry a dry cargo safely. Class "I" was for ships which on survey did not appear safe to carry dry goods but were deemed seaworthy for goods not liable to sea damage. "O" was a class of ships out of repair and not seaworthy for foreign voyages. Only two numerals were used for the classification of outfit, 1 being used for a well-found ship and 2 if the ship was not well found. In both the Green and the Red Book a vessel, after her original period of classification had expired, lapsed into an inferior class, however well kept up her hull might be or however sound her equipment. Moreover, there was neither regularity nor method in the surveys, and the surveyors were practically uncontrolled in their decisions.

The two books were in strong competition, and by 1800 the Green (or Underwriters) Book had reverted to the capital vowels and numerals for the symbols of class. The subscription to the Red Book was 8 guineas a year, against the 12 guineas for the Green Book, but in 1810, the jubilee of the latter, its subscription was reduced to 8 guineas, no doubt as much to meet the competition of the Red Book as a concession to the subscribers. Shipowners were not called upon to pay any fee for having their vessels classed, and many ships were therefore to be found in both Registers.

Both Registers carried on, in strong competition, until 1823, by which time both were in very low water financially. In that year John Marshall, a London shipowner, brought up the question of amalgamating the two Registers at a meeting of the Shipowners Society. He advocated wide reforms, such as, for instance, the representation of merchants and shipowners on the committee of the proposed new Register, where previously the two Registers had been managed by underwriters only and shipowners only, respectively. He opposed classification solely dependent upon age and place of build and disapproved of the decisions of the surveyors being uncontrolled and final.

The meeting of the Shipowners Society approved Marshall's project and advocated the setting up of a committee of inquiry on which shipowners, merchants, and underwriters should be represented. Lloyd's, however, was not co-operative. At a meeting held to consider the proposal, Benjamin Shaw, the Chairman, announced that the Committee of Lloyd's "had come to the conclusion that the proposal that Lloyd's should concur in the suggested investigation . . . was a measure which they strongly deprecated."

A report embodying a recommendation that the invitation to join the inquiry be accepted was submitted to the meeting, and Mr. Marshall, the champion of amalgamation, made an impassioned speech in which he said,

All that is now asked for is *inquiry;* and to make that efficient and to secure the approbation and support of all it is proposed that the great interests concerned shall take part in the investigation, by each appointing an equal number of persons to constitute the Committee. That this House will, on this occasion, act worthy of its character, I entertain no doubt:— celebrated, as it is, from Pole to Pole for its liberality; ever ready, as it has invariably shown itself, not only to concur, but to take the lead, in objects involving the welfare of the country, and more especially its maritime prosperity and greatness. . . . Looking, sir, at the public spirit which has ever been conspicuous in the proceedings of this House—at the tone and impulse it has at different times imparted to the country, whenever its best feelings have been properly appealed to,—recollecting, too, that the very name of Lloyd's is regarded, not at home only but also in every part of the world where the British name is known, as synonymous with everything that is liberal, just, public-spirited, and honourable,—I cannot, I will not, believe, unless the conviction is forced upon me by a decision today contrary to my expectations, that this House will on this occasion forget, or chose to lose sight of, those great principles of equity and justice towards others by which every community must regulate its conduct, or must retrograde in its character, its considerations and just consequences.

Such eloquence deserved its reward. The meeting decided with only two dissentients to nominate 24 members of whom 8 were to be elected by ballot to serve on the committee of inquiry.

Unfortunately, by the date of the ballot nearly all those nominated had withdrawn their names, and another meeting was called at which after animated discussion the opponents of the inquiry demanded a ballot the proceedings at which are best summarised by Mr. Marshall himself. He wrote,

The intense interest created by it, the feelings exhibited in its progress, and the extraordinary efforts made by most of those who so mistakenly exerted their opposition will never be forgotten by the *friends of inquiry*, who on that day supported the moderate and reasonable proposition submitted to them. Suffice it to say REASON TRIUMPHED!

The triumph was not overwhelming, however. Every counting house and coffee house in the City was dragged to procure the attendance of every subscriber who had a vote. Six hundred and seventy-nine votes were polled, and the resolution to nominate eight members to represent Lloyd's on the Committee of Inquiry was passed by 352 votes to 327.

That was in 1824. The inquiry was held, and various recommendations of a constitutional and operational nature were made and embodied in a report. A marked feature of that report was the rather pusillanimous expression of the Committee's opinion that a self-supporting Register was not practicable and that all expectations of raising a sum sufficient to cover the estimated expenditure "must, except under the sanction and authority of Parliamentary provision, prove visionary and hopeless." It was therefore proposed to seek a government subsidy which, it was suggested, might be met by a trifling duty on tonnage or a small addition to the existing duty on policies of marine insurance.

The report was submitted to a meeting held in June, 1826, at which a letter from the Board of Trade was read in which the Board expressed approval of the proposed alterations and expressed the opinion that the Lords of their Committee would be disposed to assist "in any manner which might on subsequent discussion be deemed advisable." It may be that this rather nebulous approval from official quarters had some effect in the further delay that was then experienced. The death of two of the principal leaders of the movement towards amalgamation, together with the die-hard opposition of the more conservative element at Lloyd's, also had a delaying effect. The movement dragged on, rather than progressed. Both Registers continued to lose money, and in 1829 the Committee of the Underwriters book, in an announcement notable for being the first to be headed "Lloyd's

Register of Shipping," recounted the dwindling of the Society's capital from £12,000 in 1810 to £2,000. It will be
remembered that in the jubilee year the subscription was
reduced from 12 to 8 guineas. The announcement of 1829
was to the effect that the subscription must be increased to
10 guineas.

The increase had not the desired effect. By 1833 the subscribers to the Green Book numbered only 163, and it had
only £1,000 in hand. The Red Book, with only 75 subscribers,
was still worse off. The Special Committee on the Affairs of
Lloyd's, fearing that the underwriters might be left without
any book at all, appointed a sub-committee to confer with the
committees of the two societies. A meeting was held in August,
1833, at which it was agreed that it was desirable that "an
union of the Committees of the two Registers take place
for the purpose of establishing one good and efficient Register."

Lloyd's Register

It can be said that this was, in effect, the origin of *Lloyd's
Register of British & Foreign Shipping*, as it was originally
named, for thence onward negotiations proceeded apace. In
January, 1834, a "Prospectus of the Plan for the Establishment of a New Register Book of British & Foreign Shipping"
was issued, and a fundamental change embodied in that
prospectus was the proposal that instead of being solely dependent upon the contributions of subscribers, fees, based
on tonnage, should be charged to shipowners for classification and survey of their vessels. The Board of Trade was approached, but no expectation of pecuniary assistance from
that quarter was held out.

Lloyd's, however, voted £1,000 from their funds in aid of the Society, individual underwriters subscribed an aggregate of £700, and the four insurance companies, The London Assurance, Royal Exchange, Indemnity Mutual, and Alliance, agreed to make an annual subscription of 100 guineas each. Within a few years the funds of the new Society permitted the repayment of the sum received from Lloyd's.

The first edition of *Lloyd's Register of British & Foreign Shipping* was published on 21st October, 1834. It is noted in The Annals of Lloyd's Register that

> It is somewhat surprising at this time of day to find that the use of the name "Lloyd's" in the title of the re-constituted Society was only adopted after careful consideration and not without opposition.

Early classification in the new Register followed fairly closely the practice of the earlier books. Classes were assigned for a maximum period of 12 years. The symbol "A" denoted first-class ships which had not passed a prescribed age and had been kept in the highest state of repair and efficiency. "AE" was the symbol for the second description of first class and applied to vessels which had passed the prescribed age and had not undergone the repairs required for continuation of or restoration to the "A" class but were still considered in fit condition for the safe conveyance of dry and perishable cargoes. The letter "E" designated the second class which comprised ships which, although unfit for carrying dry cargoes, were considered perfectly safe for the conveyance to all parts of the world of cargoes not in their nature liable to sea damage. The third class, denoted by the letter "I," included vessels of good constitution and fit for short voyages not out of Europe, with cargoes not subject to sea damage. The numerals 1 and 2 were used to indicate whether the condition of anchors, cables, and stores was satisfactory or otherwise.

The most important development, however, was the institution of *survey during construction* which still prevails.

From this point on the development of the system of classification would require a volume to itself. The change from the original "A1" to the current "100 A1" was the result of experience with iron ships and came into use about 1870. The basic idea was that iron vessels did not deteriorate as did those built of wood, and the new class was granted without time limit so long as on periodical survey the vessels in it were found to be in satisfactory condition. In 1853, as a result of the success which had attended the annotation "Built under Special Survey" to the classification of ships built in Canada, the Committee decided to adopt a distinguishing mark against the class of all vessels built under special survey; *i.e.*, vessels surveyed throughout the whole of their construction, and the Maltese Cross was chosen as the emblem. Vessels surveyed after completion continued to be classified and were qualified, if found to be constructed in accordance with the Register's requirements, for the highest class, but they do not carry the Maltese Cross. This practice has continued unaltered since 1853.[1]

It is impossible to go into the development of the Register's work concurrently with the development of shipping in any detail. The Society undertook the testing of chains and cables, the survey of machinery by the Society's own surveyors, where previously the certificate of any competent

[1] A page from the 1947–1948 Register is reproduced on pp. 190–191.

marine engineer was accepted. The Register kept step with all new inventions and developments and gained increasing prestige as the value of its classification became more and more recognised.

Here it should be noted that, in 1914, it was deemed that the words "British & Foreign" in the Society's title were unnecessary, and the title was changed to "Lloyd's Register of Shipping."

The Load Line

During the first 40 years of the Register, the load line of ships had not been the subject of any specific regulations, although the matter was the subject of frequent discussion. In 1870, however, controversy arose because, while the rules of the Society required awning-deck vessels to have scuppers and freeing ports at the main deck level, in order to prevent loading below the line of that deck, shipowners sometimes closed the freeing ports permanently so as to enable the vessel to be loaded below her main-deck line. In 1874, therefore, a load-line mark was made compulsory for all vessels of the awning-deck type, but a well-known line of ships declined to accept this ruling. They closed the freeing ports of their ships, and when the classification of these ships was deleted from the Register, they brought an action for damages, which they lost in both the lower court and on appeal. It was about this time that Samuel Plimsoll and other reformers began their agitation in Parliament which was eventually to result in the passing of the load-line laws. Lloyd's Register was consulted by the Board of Trade and by 1882 had drawn up, at the request of the Board, Tables of Freeboard suitable for every type of ship. By 1882 the Regis-

COR

1947-48　　LLOYD'S REGISTER,　STEAMERS & MOTORSHIPS.

No. in Book. Official No. Code Letters	Steamer's Name, Material, Rig, &c. Late Name if any. No. of Decks, &c. Special Surveys	Registered Tonnage Gross, Under deck, Net	Particulars of Classification. Character. Date of last Survey	Date When full class last seen	Equipment now expired	Built. When / By Whom / Where	Owners.	Register'd Dimensions, Deck Erections, &c. Length, Breadth, Depth.	Port of Registry. Flag.	Engines. No. & Dia. of Cylinders—Stroke. Engine Maker's Name.	Moulded depth.
22024 149975 GNLY	Corbridge ssShl.No.3-8,46 Well deck 1Dk(Stl) E.S.D. Sub.Sig. Cargo battens not fitted	1703 1295 935	✠100A1 8,46 Std q	cl. 8,46		1928 1mo S.P.Austin &Son,Ld. Sunderland Lloyd's44CP	Wm.Cory&Son,Ld. CttLDB207	255·0 37·5 16·8 P22′Q150′F21′ 440′M7i120t	London British FK4BHCm FPT70t4PT500t G.Clark,Ld.Sunderland	T.3Cy.19″,31″&53″—36″ (e) 180b 2SB.6cfgs93,ns3268	18·10 s5″8¼ 17″4¼
22025 149801 GNBK	Corchester ssShl.No.3-10,40 Well deck 1Dk(Stl) E.S.D. Sub.Sig. Cargo battens not fitted	2374 1836 1331	✠100A1 12,46 Bly ❊ Examined 12,45 BSt2,46 ✠LMC10,40	cl. 12,45		1927 4mo S.P.Austin &Son,Ld. Sunderland Lloyd's44CP CttLD	Wm.Cory&Son,Ld. B234′384t side tank	265·0 41·7 19·0 Q165′F31′ k⁴ in ER168t FPT	London British FK4BHCm 105t4PT298t G.Clark,Ld.Sunderland	T.3Cy.20½″,35″&57″—39″(r) 180b Q155′F31′	21″1 s6″7¾ 19″1¼
22026 140718 GBTI	Corcrest (exHopecrest) ssShl2ndDk-2,46 Well deck 1Dk(Stl) E.S.D. Sub.Sig. Cargo battens not fitted	2373 1363 1337	✠100A1 6,46 Shl s BSt6,46	cl. 4,46		1918 6mo Swan,Hun- ter&Wigham Richardson, Ld.Sunderland Lloyd's44CP	Wm.Cory&Son,Ld. CttLDB286′58t side tanks in engine space 206t FPT	285·8 41·5 19·1 P94′Q122′B20′F31′	London British 4BHCm Richardson,Ld.Nwc.	T.3Cy.22″,35″&68″—39″ (r) 180b 2SB.6cfgs107,ns94204 Swan,Hunter&Wigham	21″4 s6″4¾ 19″2
22027 149129 GLKR	Cordale (exHorsley-87) ssShl.No.3-4,88 1Dk(Stl) E.S.D. Sub.Sig. Cargo battens not fitted	2143 1853 1244	✠100A1 7,46 Shl s Examined7,46 ✠LMC	cl. 3,45		1925 7mo Smith's DockCo.Ld. Middlesbro' Lloyd's44CP	Wm.Cory&Son,Ld. CttLDB231′644	280·0 41·6 20·1 292·2(o.l.) P21′B49′F26′ FPT60t4PT717t	London British FK4BHCm Smith'sDockCo.Ld.Mdb.	T.3Cy.20½″,35″&64″—39″(r) 180b 2SB.6cfgs103,ns59947	22″3 s3″2¼ 19″5
22028 144239 GDRK	Cordillera ssGls.No.3-10,33 3Dks 4thDk in'foreholds D.F. E.S.D. Platform Dk in Nos.4&5 holds	6865 6573 4248	✠100A1 Liv at Shelter dc with freeboard 8,46 Examined8,46 ✠LMC MS3,37 BSt8,46 Ref.Mchy. See separate section (Fitted for oil fuel)	cl. 4,45		1920 10mo ShortBros. Ld. Sunderland Lloyd's44CP	DonaldsonLine,Ld. (DonaldsonBros.& Black,Ld.Mgrs.) CttLDB344′1198t	419·0 54·8 35·7 434·9(o.l.) F778t4PT261t	Glasgow British FK Cem TBHto5h.dk.	3steam turbinesDRgeared 200b N.E.MarineEngCoLd.Nwc	38″3 (t)s10·10¾ 8623N 27″8
22029	Corduba D.F. E.S.D. GyC. OilEng. Mchy.Aft Ref.Mchy. 2Dks Elec.welded Cruiser Stern	3802 — 2121		F.P. above 150° F		1944 PennsylvaniaShipyards,Inc. Beaumont, Tex.	UnitedStates Maritime Commission	323·9 50·1 26·5 P90′F38′	Beaumont, Tex. U.d.States WB	OilEngines 2S.C.SA 6Cy.21⅜″-29″ NordbergMfg.Co. Milwaukee,Wis.	R
22030 163832 GWWY	Corfell Sub.Sig. E.S.D. Sub.Sig. Mchy.Aft Cruiser Stern	1802 1354 1016	✠100A1 1Dk			1934 S.P.Austin &Son,Ld. Sunderland	ConcreteMaritime, Ld.(Wm.Cory& Son,Ld.Mgrs.)	257·0 39·5 16·7 Q150′F2½′	London British WB	T.3Cy.16½″,28″&47″—33″ N.E.MarineEng.Co.LdStd	C

Fig. 6. Page from *Lloyd's Register*, 1947–1948.

22031 180005 GDJX	**Corfen** *Mchy.Aft* 1*Dk* *CruiserStern* *Cargo battens not fitted*	1867 1344 986	✠100A1 7,45 ✠LMC11,44	Shl	*q*	OG	1944 11mo *Lloyd*	Hall,Russell&Co.Ld Aberdeen '*sA4CP*	CoryColliers,Ld. (Wm.Cory&Sons, Ld.*Mgrs.*) *CellDB214'*	257·0|39·5|16·7 264·9(O.L.) Q150'F25' FK 500t*MT9'*166t*FPT*	London British 6*BH* 158t*APT*20t	T.3Cy.16½",27½"&46"-33" 200lb FD (*s*) 190MN 2SB(Spt),6*cf*,GS77,HS2880 D.Rowan&Co Ld.Gls	18 " 9 s6 " 0½ 17 " 4½	
22032 165601 GDDW	**Corferry** *ss*Shl.No.2-45 E.S.D. 1*Dk* Sub.Sig *CruiserStern* *Mchy.Aft* *Cargo battens not fitted*	1788 1344 1003	✠100A1 8,46 BS8,46 ✠LMC7,45	Bly	*q*	CL 7,46	1937 11mo *Lloyd*	Burntislnd S.B.Co.Ld. Burntisland '*sA4CP*	Wm.Cory&Son,Ld. *CellDB214'*500t	257·0|39·5|16·7 265·0(O.L.) Q150'F25' FK *MT9'*166t *FPT*158t	London British 4*BHCem* *APT*21t	T.3Cy.16",25"&45"-33" 220lb FD (*s*) 176MN 2SB(Spt),6*cf*,GS49,HS2506 N.E.MarineEng.Co.Ld.Sld	18 " 9 s6 " 1 17 " 4	
22033 163476 MBVN	**Corfirth** E.S.D. *Mchy.Aft* *ss*Lgn.-4,46 *Well deck* Sub.Sig. 1*Dk* *CruiserStern* *Cargo battens not fitted*	1803 1355 1016	✠100A1 2,47 ✠LMC4,46	Sld	*q*	CL 11,46	1934 5mo *Lloyd*	S.P.Austin &Son,Ld. Sunderland '*sA4CP*	Wm.Cory&Son,Ld. *CellDB214'*492	257·0|39·5|16·7 Q150'F25' FK t*MT9'*164t *FPT*159	London British 4*BHptCem* t*APT*15t	T.3Cy.16½",28"&47"-33"(*s*) 220lb 171MN 2SB(Spt),6*cf*,GS76,HS2854 N.E.MarineEng.Co.Ld.Sld	18 " 9 s6 " 0½ 17 " 4	
22034 163484 GWTD	**Corfleet** S.D.E. *ss*Shl.-11,46 Sub.Sig. 1*Dk* *Mchy.Aft* *CruiserStern* *Cargo battens not fitted*	1803 1355 1015	✠100A1 11,46 ✠LMC11,46	Shl	*q*	CL 10,46	1934 6mo *Lloyd*	S.P.Austin &Son,Ld. Sunderland '*sA4CP*	ConcreteMaritime, Ld.(Wm.Cory& Son,Ld.*Mgrs.*) *CellDB214'*	257·0|39·5|16·7 Q150'F25' FK 492t*MT9'*164t*FPT*	London British 4*BHptCem* 159t*APT*15t	T.3Cy 16½",28"&47"-33"(*s*) 220lb 171MN 2SB(Spt),6*cf*,GS76,HS2854 N.E.MarineEng.Co Ld.Sld	18 " 9 s 6 " 0½ 17 " 4	
22035 180886 GLYB	**Corflow** (*ex*EmpireLowlander-46) *Mchy.Aft* 1*Dk* *CruiserStern*	2159 1509 1114					1946	J.Crown& Sons,Ld. Sunderland	CoryColliers,Ld. (Wm.Cory&Son, Ld.*Mgrs.*)	273·0|41·0|17·4	London British *WB*	T.3Cy.17",27"&48"-36" N.E.MarineEng.Co.(1938) Ld.Sld.		C
22036 168271 BDRX	**Corfoss** *ss*Sld.-7,46 E.S.D. 1*Dk* *Mchy.Aft* *CruiserStern* *Cargo battens not fitted*	1849 1344 990	✠100A1 7,46 ✠LMC7,46	Sld	*q*	OG 3,45	1942 3mo *Lloyd*	Burntislnd S.B.Co.Ld. Burntisland '*sA4CP*	Wm.Cory&Son,Ld. *CellDB214'*500t	257·0|39·5|16·7 264·9(O.L.) Q150'F24' FK *MT9'*166t*FPT*158t	London British 4*BHptCem* *ptAsp* *APT*21t	T.3Cy.16½",27½"&46"-33" 200lb FD (*s*) 245MN 2SB,(Spt)6*cf*,GS77,HS4120 D.Rowan&Co.Ld.Gls.	18 " 8 s 6 " 0¾ 17 " 4¾	
22037 162643 GRNW	**Corfu** TwinSc 3*Dks*(*Stl-Weather dk* ws) 4*th dk*(*Stl*)*in forward holds* D.F. E.S.D. Radar *CruiserStern* *Fitted for oil fuel*	14170 11383 7665	✠ 9,35 ✠ Ref.Mchy. (*See separate section*)	Lon	*j*†		1931 9mo	A.Stephen &Sons,Ld. Glasgow	P.& O.Stm.Nav.Co *Cell*	522·5|71·4|33·1 B246'F76' FK *DB*448'2568t*FPT*7	London British 9*BHptCem* *Coll.,toWdk* 0t*APT*140t	6 steam turbinesSR geared to 2 sc. shafts A Stephen&Sons.Ld.Gls.	46 " 0	MT till 1.48
22038 161301 GFZB	**Corglen** E.S.D. *ss*Sld.No.2-38 Sub.Sig. 1*Dk*(*Stl*) *Mchy.Aft* *Well deck* *Cargo battens not fitted*	2822 2201 1632	✠100A1 2,47 Examined2,47 BS2,47 ✠LMC8,38	Shl	*l*	CL 6,45	1929 9mo *Lloyd*	Cowpen D.D.&S.B. Co.Ld. Blyth '*sA4CP*	Wm.Cory&Son,Ld. *CellDB250'*747t	306·4|44·2|19·9 Q186'F30' FK *MT10'*347t *FPT*13	London British 6*BHptCem* 6t*APT*17t	T.3Cy.21½",36"&60"-39"(*s*) 180lb 259MN 2SB(Spt)8*of*,GS128,HS4196 G.Clark,Ld.Sunderland	22 " 0 s 7 " 0¾ 19 " 10	
22039														

14d‡ COR

Fig. 6. (*Continued*)

ter was ready to assign freeboards to all types of vessels, classed or not, and it is noteworthy that from thence onward, before any legislative action had been taken, many shipowners did in fact ask for freeboard to be assigned to their vessels. It was not, however, until 1890 that the load-line laws were passed, and an important feature of the bill in which those laws were initially drafted was that it accepted Lloyd's Register, as well as the Board of Trade, as an authority empowered to allot load lines to ships. Since the whole basis of calculating freeboard had, in fact, been created by the Register, this was only right and proper.

The bill embodying the new law had already been passed by the House of Commons when certain shipowners and shipbuilders, particularly those on the Clyde, became apprehensive lest the virtual monopoly thus given to Lloyd's Register should prove "a limitation which might well have had the effect of perpetuating indefinitely the classification rules of these days and at the same time grievously hindering further progress." [1]

The British Corporation Register

These Clydeside interests therefore created a new Register to be known as the British Corporation Register and pursued their aim so energetically that in the House of Lords the bill was amended to recognise the new Corporation, and also the British Committee of the Bureau Veritas (the French classification society), as additional load-line-assigning authorities.

In 1890, therefore, after a lapse of 56 years, there were

[1] Gilbert J. Innes, Chairman at 50th Annual Meeting of British Corporation of Shipping.

again two competing registers in the United Kingdom. It may be that Lloyd's Register was, at that time, ultra-conservative, but it must be borne in mind that it never departed from the very high standard of absolute staunchness and seaworthiness which had made its name famous throughout the world. Perhaps it would be better to say that in the nineties Lloyd's Register was content to survey and classify ships designed by naval architects and built by shipbuilders, and took no active part in the development of new design and new methods of construction, while the British Corporation showed greater enterprise in giving active assistance in the creation of new forms of hulls and new methods of propulsion. The first vessel classed by the British Corporation, the *Turret*, was not a success in herself, but the experience gained with her undoubtedly had its effect on ship design in the future. Innes, in the speech to which reference is made above, said,

> The logical outcome of this flexibility was that an end was ultimately made of the indefensible practice of building ships to dodge grades in rules. Today every classification society conforms to our principle that there should be only one standard—the highest for the service for which the ship is designed—and owners and builders do not now find such amazing contrasts between the Rules of the different societies as existed in the early years of the century.

Beyond all question, the creation of the new Corporation and the competition it offered had the effect of keeping Lloyd's Register on its toes and of combatting any tendency to over-conservatism that may have existed in the years towards the end of last century, when tradition and long-established custom were regarded with a reverence that seems to have been over-rated viewed from the standpoint of these progressive days. Evidence of how the two rival societies kept abreast of the times is to be found in the fact that they both developed rules for the classification of aircraft when carriage by air became a commercial proposition rather than a scientific experiment. In all directions the element of competition undoubtedly operated to the advancement of the shipping industry not only in the United Kingdom but throughout the maritime world. By the 1940's, however, a strong movement for the amalgamation of Lloyd's Register and the British Corporation Register came into being, and after what at first appeared to be a definite breakdown in the negotiations towards this end, success was achieved in 1949, and the two great institutions were merged into one.

To sum up, Lloyd's Register, supported by shipping, commercial, and insurance interests, is not an integral part of Lloyd's but is so closely allied with Lloyd's as to be one of its most essential adjuncts. The fact that a ship holds the highest class of Lloyd's Register is sufficient to ensure that she is regarded by underwriters as staunch and seaworthy. Her trade, the record of her owners, and other factors may affect her rating for insurance purposes, but her class in Lloyd's Register is accepted as conclusive evidence of her structural soundness and efficiency. On the other hand the loss of her class by a vessel is sufficient in itself to make that vessel a very difficult insurance proposition. But the function of Lloyd's Register is not by any means only to provide underwriters with a guarantee of staunchness and seaworthiness. Classification in Lloyd's Register puts the seal on a ship for the purpose of carriage of passengers and cargo, it enhances her value for sale, and it is the anchor upon which shipowners themselves rely to hold their vessels fast to the standard of the highest efficiency of design and maintenance.

Chapter 7. LLOYD'S AND THE SECOND WORLD WAR

The outbreak of war in September, 1939, had a profound effect on both business and practice at Lloyd's. To take the major physical effects first, it brought about a dispersal and a concentration of the marine-insurance market at the same time. Fear of air raids had previously led Lloyd's to make arrangements for the evacuation of the Policy Signing Office and other administrative departments immediately war broke out. The majority of brokers had also made similar arrangements for their staffs other than those engaged in the placing of risks and other active brokerage transactions, and since Lloyd's had acquired premises in film studios at Pinewood, in Bucks, brokers' evacuated offices tended to centre around that district. This arrangement necessitated a shuttle-car service by which policies and other documents could be carried daily between Lloyd's and Pinewood and between the London and evacuated offices of the brokers, and it says much for the organisation of these services that they operated admirably from the outset.

Another development arising out of the same circumstances was the application of microphotography to the keeping of records. A number of brokers installed apparatus by which slips were photographed on strips of film similar to those used in cinema work. By this means records of a very large number of slips could be kept in a very small space and stored where they would be comparatively safe from enemy attack. When required for reference, the film of the slip in question could easily be projected onto a screen showing it enlarged to easily readable size. The advantage of this system was that it preserved not only the essential details of every risk in small compass and enabled the records to be stored in safe places, but also that it preserved in facsimile the actual slip on which a risk had been placed so that, in the event of the original document being destroyed, a precise and un-challengeable duplicate was available showing even the under-writers' initials as they appeared on the original.

Co-operation

So much for dispersal, but there was also concentration because fear of air attack caused the majority of the marine-insurance companies which had underwriting rooms and offices in the streets adjoining Lloyd's to move into Lloyd's building. Some were able to obtain their own offices in the building; others became the guests of companies with per-manent offices therein, and it was an example of the solidar-ity of the market that competing companies willingly gave house room to each other and accepted the inconveniences of overcrowding without hesitation. Even a greater indica-tion of solidarity was the system by which, for some little time after the outbreak of war, a number of companies entered into an arrangement by which one underwriter acted for the whole group.

There were two main groups of this nature, the idea being that with the possibility of communications being gravely interrupted there would always be an organisation through which business could be carried on. Even if a number of individual underwriters were prevented from reaching the City, there would always be one competent to act for the others. It is understood that the idea of appointing a single underwriter to act for the whole of Lloyd's Underwriters was also considered for the same reason, but in the event it proved that this was not necessary. Moreover, as soon as it became apparent that the scale of devastation by enemy attack was far less heavy than had been anticipated, normal business operations were resumed, although the majority of companies which had moved into Lloyd's Building remained there for underwriting purposes.

The Shelter

After the crisis of 1938, the Committee of Lloyd's began to prepare a safe shelter deep down below the main building, and hundreds if not thousands of tons of cement and steel went to make a set of apartments so well protected that they are believed to be secure against even the heaviest bombs. These apartments, equipped with air conditioning, emergency lighting, telephones, and all the necessities of their purpose, were initially intended as refuges to which those at Lloyd's could resort during air attack, but when air raids intensified after the collapse of France, arrangements were made by which the business normally transacted in the Underwriting Room could be transferred to the shelter. Every underwriter in The Room was allotted a seat in the underground apartments, and adjacent apartments were set aside for the marine-insurance companies which had premises in Lloyd's building. On a signal that enemy aircraft were approaching, everybody in Lloyd's building proceeded by a pre-arranged route to the shelter, and within less than 10 minutes the market was reconstituted below ground and was carrying on its business secure from disaster. During the Battle of Britain in 1940 and the "Blitz" of 1941, and again during the flying-bomb attacks of 1944, the foresight of the Committee of Lloyd's in providing this means of carrying on business safe from enemy attack was amply justified.

The American Trust Fund

One of the most important developments coincident with the outbreak of war was the creation of Lloyd's *American Trust Fund* in the United States of America. Its creation was announced in the following official statement issued on August 30th, 1939:

> For some time past the Committee of Lloyd's have had under consideration the desirability of vesting the U.S.A. Dollar premiums of Lloyd's Underwriters in an American trustee.
>
> Hitherto Lloyd's Underwriters have maintained U.S.A. Dollar balances in the form of cash and investments in the U.S.A., but under the trust deeds applicable to the premiums executed by them, all premiums from wherever emanating, and in whatever currency they are payable have been vested in trustees in England.
>
> These trust deeds have now been varied so as to vest the premiums in respect of U.S.A. dollar insurances in the City Bank Farmers Trust Co. of New York as trustees in order to safeguard these premiums for the payment of claims arising under the insurances for which they have been primarily received.

Undoubtedly the primary reason for the creation of this trust fund was not any apprehension that Lloyd's underwriters might not be able to meet their commitments, but to ensure that there should be always immediately available, in the United States, funds out of which claims on American insurances could be met without transfer of monies from England.

Two considerations affected the situation. The first was that in view of the then unknown perils of modern warfare communications might be so interrupted that relations between underwriters and brokers in London and their representatives in America might be difficult, and the other was the necessity of providing a fund which would not be subject to the requirements of the Government in respect of foreign currencies during the war. It should be understood that this arrangement was made with the full consent and approval of the British Government who realised the importance of maintaining the full efficiency of Lloyd's service abroad and the necessity for the provision of funds out of which obligations could be met immediately they were due. Later in the war the English marine-insurance companies also created a Dollar Trust Fund in the United States, but on different lines.

War Risks

After the crisis of 1938, as a preliminary to the setting up of a Government War Risks Insurance Office, marine underwriters at Lloyd's and the companies had entered into an arrangement by which they reinsured all their war-risk business with a *Pool* created by themselves. All the business reinsured in this Pool was, in turn, reinsured by the Government, but against King's Enemy risks only, leaving the Pool to carry such war risks as were not King's Enemy risks. Thus, in effect, every underwriter, as a member of the Pool, enjoyed a share of all the war-risk business placed in the market, but his net liability was only for war risks other than King's Enemy risks, *i.e.*, risks in which the enemies of Great Britain were not concerned. The Pool made a profit consisting of the difference between the premiums paid into it and the premiums paid by it for the Government's reinsurance, and each member of the Pool received a share of this profit commensurate to the volume of business contributed by him to the Pool.

Immediately war broke out, however, the Pool ceased to function because the Government set up their War Risks Insurance Office in premises immediately opposite Lloyd's. By tacit agreement, underwriters in the open market refrained from competing with the Government office for war risks on voyages to and from the United Kingdom. This arrangement, which persisted until April, 1945, gave the Government a virtual monopoly of war risks on imports and exports to and from the United Kingdom, leaving Lloyd's and the marine-insurance companies with war risks on cross voyages [1] as their main source of war-risk business. Even cross voyages were insurable with the Government office from October, 1939, onwards, but with regard to this business there was no tacit agreement as to non-competition with the Government. The result was that, during the bad times up to the middle of 1942, the Government's rates were generally lower than those of the open market, but as the war situation at sea improved the rates of the market tended to become lower than those of the Government, sometimes substantially so.

[1] A "cross voyage" in English market parlance is one with neither terminus in the United Kingdom, for example, New York to Calcutta.

The system of fixing market war-risk rates, while attaining primary importance during the war, really dates back to the Italo-Abyssinian affair of 1935. Then, when war perils became active rather than potential for the first time since the First World War, certain underwriters, mainly those of the leading marine-insurance companies, compiled schedules of rates for voyages within the zone of active hostilities, thus saving brokers the trouble of obtaining individual quotations for every war risk they had to cover. These rates largely ruled the market, and very soon, by collaboration between Lloyd's and the Institute of London Underwriters, the organisation of the marine-insurance companies, market schedules of war-risk rates were adopted to which both Lloyd's Underwriters and the companies were pledged by tacit agreement. This system of rating war risks by schedule might have been abandoned but for the fact that the Sino-Japanese "incident," the trouble in Palestine, and the Spanish Civil War made it necessary to maintain active war-risk insurances and so kept the schedule system in being. This was fortunate for in the crisis of 1938, and again when war broke out, the market was organised for the insurance of war risks at standard rates. While on occasion this system was in danger of breaking down by reason of unrest among certain underwriters who were inclined to break away from the schedule system, it proved so indispensable that, whenever a breakdown threatened, wiser counsels prevailed, and the system was preserved, with certain modifications. Similarly when the Government set up the War Risks Insurance Office at the outbreak of war, the schedule system was adopted. This was in contrast with the practice during the First World War, when, for the greater part of the time, the Government Office had a flat rate for war risks on all voyages. The disadvantage of this system was that it permitted underwriters at Lloyd's and the marine-insurance companies to write war risks on the safer voyages at rates lower than those of the Government Office, leaving the latter to carry the worst risks at the flat rate, whatever it might be. The fact that both the open market and the Government made substantial profits out of marine war risks during the First World War in no way alters the principle that it is undesirable that private underwriters should be in a favourable position owing to what amounts to a hidden subsidy, the hidden subsidy being the dumping ground provided by the Government Office for the worst risks. The system of the Second World War, outlined above, was far more satisfactory although it had its disadvantages.

The Government Office transacted war-risk business only, purely marine business remaining the prerogative of Lloyd's and the marine-insurance companies. The open market, which these two units compose, was in danger of being starved of marine business, however, because virtually all essential imports had been taken over by the Ministries of Food and Supply for the purpose of equitable distribution among the people and the most efficient use of the raw materials of munitions of war. It has never been the custom of the English Government to insure its property, but after discussions between market leaders and representatives of the two Ministries, it was realised that the non-insurance of the bulk of the nation's imports would create a hardship on underwriters, and so it was arranged that practically all the imports controlled by the two Ministries should be insured against marine risks under one vast comprehensive policy.

This policy, an *open cover* or permanent contract, was underwritten by the whole market, Lloyd's and the companies. Every marine syndicate at Lloyd's and each company took an agreed percentage of the risk on every shipment insured for the account of the Ministries so that the risk was distributed equitably over the whole market. The figures of the contract were colossal. In the first year the amounts declared to underwriters exceeded £444,000,000, and the premiums were over £1,650,000. The sums insured on some interests ran into tens of millions, the wool imports were covered for nearly £60,000,000, and oils and fats for over £33,000,000. In later years the total insured reached between £600,000,-000 and £700,000,000.

The contract was expressed in a single policy, signed by authorised representatives on behalf of Lloyd's, the London and Liverpool companies, and the underwriters in Glasgow who still carry on business as individual insurers on the Lloyd's system, forming syndicates and signing policies as is done at Lloyd's. Individual shipments insured under the contract were often very large. The limit covered in any one vessel was £1,500,000 but whilst it was never reached during the war some declarations were not far short of the total, while after the war the total was in fact exceeded in the case of some shipments. The contract was, in fact, an omnibus insurance of practically the whole of the nation's import trade, excluding certain interests used solely in the war effort, such as petrol and lubricating oil.

Another of these mass insurances was the vast hull policy effected on Norwegian tonnage which came under the control of the Allied nations. When Norway was invaded, the British Government broadcast wireless instructions to the masters of Norwegian ships at sea to put into the nearest

British or neutral port. In order to reassure the masters that the interests of their shipowners were being protected, they were informed that their vessels would be fully insured against both war and marine risks until they had safely arrived, irrespective of any insurances that had previously been placed. This was essential because the over-running of Norway had placed the Norwegian insurance industry under German control, and it was obvious that, if a Norwegian vessel passed under the control of the English Government, the Norwegian companies, dominated by the invading enemy, would be unable to pay any claims that might have been incurred.

This assurance was given before any precise arrangements had been made to implement it. Of course, the war risk could be covered by the War Risks Insurance Office, which was the Government's own concern, but no such machinery existed for covering the marine risk, and so the Government asked the marine-insurance market to take the matter over. Again the principle of mass insurance was applied. Every underwriter at Lloyd's and all the marine-insurance companies transacting hull business took an agreed proportion of the risk, and a single policy for over £100,000,000 was issued to cover the vessels. When the Norwegian Shipping and Trade Mission was set up in London and took control of the Norwegian tonnage which had thus come under the control of the Allied nations, the insurance was continued year by year, and similar insurances were also effected on Danish and Dutch vessels which had come under the control of the Allied nations.

These mass insurances are, of course, only wartime expedients. They are the very negation of underwriting as practiced at Lloyd's for they eliminate individual judgment and the selection of risks which has built up Lloyd's to the great institution it is. Underwriters were faced with a "take it or leave it" proposition. Many of them disliked the principle involved intensely, but recognising that it was in the national interest that they should participate in these insurances, they did so without demur. It is believed that not one instance of an underwriter failing to co-operate was experienced.

Areas Occupied by the Enemy

Many difficulties were created in the marine-insurance market by the over-running of the northern European countries with which Lloyd's Underwriters had many important business connections. For one thing, when a country came under the domination of the enemy, all business transactions with nationals of that country became prohibited by the "Trading with the Enemy Act." In many cases substantial sums were owed to Lloyd's Underwriters by nationals of these countries, and sums were also owed to these nationals for claims. Shipowners often pay their premiums on the deferred system, paying one-fourth of the annual premiums in cash and the other three-fourths in equal quarterly instalments. Unpaid instalments on such transactions became irrecoverable from shipowners domiciled in enemy-occupied countries as did premiums on cargo business and reinsurances which fell due to be paid after the enemy had occupied the country in which the assured was domiciled. Similarly underwriters could not pay claims to any parties domiciled in enemy-occupied territory. For a time the situation created grave concern because in English law premiums on marine-insurance contracts placed through a broker are payable by the broker, irrespective of whether he has been paid by the assured. Technically the brokers who had placed the business affected by the German conquest of European countries were responsible to the underwriters who had written the business, without any hope of obtaining the premiums from their clients. Obviously the situation could not be dealt with in the letter of the law, and arrangements were eventually made by which the whole question of these unpaid premiums was left in abeyance to be settled after the war in the light of the situation as it then would be found to exist. To prevent any further complications of a similar nature, however, underwriters adopted the *Payment of Premiums Clause* making the acceptance of risk, which normally is dependent upon the initialling of the slip by an underwriter, dependent upon the payment of the premium within 10 days of the date of attachment, in the case of risks for periods of time, and in the case of voyage policy, within 10 days of the date of despatch of notification to the assured of the provisional placing of the risk.

Missing Vessels

In August, 1941, there was a development of some importance which was eventually to result in collaboration between the English and American markets. This was the setting up of a Committee of Arbitration to deal with cases in which there was doubt as to whether the loss of a "missing" vessel should fall on the war- or the marine-risk policy. During the First World War there was a certain amount of litigation over such cases, and always in time of war there is the problem of whether a vessel posted as "missing" has been lost by a war or a marine peril. Even on a voyage on which no bad weather would be experienced, and through waters known to be infested with enemy vessels, absolute certainty as to the cause of loss is impossible. However, a committee supplemented by machinery for arbitration can apportion probabilities, and settlements can be made by agreement on the basis of such apportionments, whereas in law there can be no apportionment, and a hard-and-fast decision in favour of the war or the marine underwriters is unavoidable. This Committee has operated with outstanding success, and it was not surprising that American underwriters adopted a similar system dealing with missing-vessel losses, by agreement between American underwriters and the War Shipping Administration (an American governmental bureau) with regard to settling claims on missing ships and also in cases where it was not immediately apparent whether the war- or the marine-risk underwriters should be liable.

In 1943, a further agreement, by which British underwriters became virtual parties to this American agreement, extended the principle of settling such claims by arbitration to all business in which American and English interests were concerned, as, for instance, where the war risk was covered by the War Shipping Administration and the marine risk with English insurers.

Ship Warrants

A similar development occurred in connection with the *ship warrant warranty*, which was a provision incorporated in marine-insurance policies on ships by which the protection of the policy was nullified if the vessel did not have a ship warrant, by which the British Government set their seal of approval on a vessel and marked their acceptance of the fact that she was neither owned, controlled, nor in any way associated with enemy interests.

The entry of America into the war necessitated a readjustment of the requirements with regard to ship warrants in relation to insurance, and in February, 1942, the ship warrant warranty was amended and reissued under the somewhat clumsy and prolix title of "British Ship Warrant and United States of America Ship Warrant Warranty (1942)," in which the requirements that a vessel must have a ship warrant or be otherwise approved by the Government were extended to include vessels either registered under the American flag or otherwise approved by the American authorities as being entitled to the privileges of an American ship-warrant holder. The basic idea of this warranty was that no vessel which was in any way associated with enemy interests should benefit by British or American insurance. The warranty was, in fact, a weapon of economic warfare placed in the hands of underwriters by the governments of the Allied nations and an important factor in the blockade of enemy countries. It meant that unless an insured vessel held either a British or American ship warrant, or its equivalent, any insurances effected on that vessel with insurers of the Allied nations were inoperative and afforded no protection to the assured.

This was only one of the ways in which the American and British markets collaborated during the wars, and there were many others. The two markets were always in consultation over the question of war-risk rating, and in so far as cargo war risks on voyages to or from North and Central

America were concerned, the rates of the London market were kept in close approximation of those fixed by American underwriters.

Combined Marine Surcharges

A remarkable and revolutionary development in the cargo-insurance market during the war was that which eventually led to the *Combined Marine Surcharges.* It was apparent, in the earliest days of the war, that the purely marine hazards of overseas trade, as distinct from those covered by the war-risk policy, were increased by the prevailing conditions at sea. The extinction of coastal lights, the removal of buoys, the dimming of a ship's navigational lights, the necessity of sailing on routes other than those customary to the trade—all these undoubtedly made voyages more perilous than in times of peace. In January, 1940, therefore, a market agreement supported by Lloyd's and the marine-insurance companies brought into being a system of cargo surcharges which, initially, were simple and comparatively small additional rates added to the basis rates at which the insured cargoes would be insured in times of peace. These rates were expressed in a schedule which in the beginning was one of a very few items, a basic surcharge of ⅛ per cent being fixed for major voyages and lower rates for local and coastal voyages.

The entry of Italy into the war, which virtually closed the Mediterranean to British shipping, involved the deviation of vessels bound to and from the East via the Cape route, and to offset the increased perils of this route, an additional premium was charged on cargo in ships making the deviation. Then, in May, 1942, the adoption of special

wartime clauses giving cargo extended transit cover resulted in yet a further additional premium being charged in
cases where the assured elected to insure under these clauses
which, at that time, were optional. Thus, by 1943, the cargo
market was operating under a system of rating which comprised the basic rate, plus the simple surcharge of January,
1940, plus the additional premium for deviation via the Cape
route, where necessary, plus the additional premium for the
extended transit clauses when they were embodied in the
policy. The system was complex and laborious, and in May,
1943, by a general market agreement, all these various additional premiums were merged into the Combined Marine
Surcharges.

These surcharges were expressed in a schedule of rates
which were in four columns under headings applying to
the various types of policy conditions in common use. The
first column was for the ordinary "With Average" and "Free
of Particular Average" policies, which cover fortuitous maritime perils but exclude extraneous risks. The other columns
contained rates applicable to policy conditions of a more
comprehensive nature, from the ordinary "With Average"
or "Free of Particular Average" including theft and pilferage, up to the fullest policy conditions obtainable. Initially
rates were fixed for individual voyages, additional rates being added in successive issues of the schedule until eventually the booklet of rates became one of a great number of
items including practically every voyage likely to be made
in overseas trade and a very large number of coastal and
local voyages. As conditions at ports worsened during the
war, the surcharge rates tended to become higher and higher,
especially for voyages on which the risk of theft and pilferage

had become abnormal, and those to ports where congestion due to war conditions resulted in great accumulations of cargo, largely unprotected and exposed not only to the depredations of thieves but to damage by the elements. Indeed, the surcharge rates were in many cases very considerably higher than the basic rates to which they were added and which represented the rates at which the risk would be insured in normal conditions. The result of the disproportion between the surcharge rates and the basic rates made the surcharge system in effect a tariff. The system curbed, in fact practically eliminated competition, for the market was pledged to observe the surcharge schedule though it was quite foreign to the tradition of the British market which has always clung tenaciously to its right to freedom of competition by individual rating.

The surcharge system was, however, loyally supported by the whole market during the war as a necessary evil. Soon after the war ended, however, there sprung into being a movement towards the abolition of the surcharges and the resumption of individual rating. The movement was particularly noticeable at Lloyd's while the companies, as a whole, were in favour of retaining the surcharges for the time being, although it was generally admitted that eventually they must disappear. Controversy raged over this matter, not only in the columns of the shipping and financial press, but openly at the annual conferences of the International Marine Insurance Union and in the speeches of the chairmen of underwriting organisations and of the marine-insurance companies, at annual meetings.

In May, 1949, it was announced that the Combined-marine-surcharge system would be discontinued as from July 1st of that year, and the change-over from a virtual tariff to free underwriting was accomplished with far less dislocation of business and certainly far less in the way of rate cutting than had generally been anticipated. The system served a very useful purpose during the war. Undoubtedly it kept cargo business on a profitable basis while it lasted, but it was only a wartime expedient and even those who considered that it was abandoned too soon were not really sorry to see it go.

British Insurance Communications Office

One of the gravest problems of marine-insurance business during the war concerned the transmission of shipping information. It was essential that in transacting business with interests in other countries, details of voyages, ships' names, cargoes carried, and often precise sailing dates should be mentioned in letters and other documents. The volume of business passing between the United States and England was enormous, and ships in the transatlantic trade were exposed to the gravest perils of enemy attack. If it so happened that an enemy submarine or commerce raider captured mail carried in a ship in that trade, there would immediately become available to the enemy intelligence departments details of voyages and sailings which would be of inestimable value to those directing the attacks upon our shipping. On the other hand, without such information essential insurance business could not be carried on.

To solve this problem, the *British Insurance Communications Office* was set up, and by means of this office details in an unbreakable code giving all the necessary particulars could be sent. The code was such that even if the enemy captured documents containing vital information it would avail him nothing, and the fact that after the office was set up in no case was there any possibility that a loss by enemy action resulted from information obtained from insurance documents taken from captured vessels is proof of this.

Lloyd's prospered during the war. Considerable profits were made, but these were not disproportionate to the immense volume of business transacted, nor to the important part played in the nation's affairs by the security given, by Lloyd's Underwriters, to overseas commerce. The risks run by those who afforded this security were also very considerable. During the first half of 1942, the losses incurred through submarine attacks on our shipping were so great that at the end of June it is probable that the market as a whole had incurred an underwriting loss. That during the second half of the year our anti-submarine measures together with reasonable increases in rates had restored the fortunes of the market was largely fortuitous. The important point is that, in bad times without panic and in good times without exultation, Lloyd's Underwriters, and the marine companies too, continued to give the security of insurance so essential to the nation's overseas trade, for without that security private enterprise could not face the risk of crippling loss from the perils of the seas and the King's enemies which assume such threatening proportions in times of war.

INDEX